Focus

Hack Your Productivity for Massive Success

(A Quick-start Guide to Mastering Your Attention Ignoring Distractions)

Carlos McClure

Published By **Simon Dough**

Carlos McClure

Focus: Hack Your Productivity for Massive Success (A Quick-start Guide to Mastering Your Attention Ignoring Distractions)

ISBN 978-1-998927-07-4

No part of this guidebook shall be reproduced in any form without permission in writing from the publisher except in the case of brief quotations embodied in critical articles or reviews.

Legal & Disclaimer

The information contained in this book is not designed to replace or take the place of any form of medicine or professional medical advice. The information in this book has been provided for educational & entertainment purposes only.

The information contained in this book has been compiled from sources deemed reliable, and it is accurate to the best of the Author's knowledge; however, the Author cannot guarantee its accuracy and validity and cannot be held liable for any errors or omissions. Changes are periodically made to this book. You must consult your doctor or get professional medical advice before using any of the suggested remedies, techniques, or information in this book.

Table Of Contents

Chapter1: Techniques to Improve Concentration

In this financial ruin we will cover a few techniques and techniques that will help you enhance your consciousness. These are smooth however powerful steps which will skip an prolonged way to beneficial useful resource you consciousness on the responsibilities handy with out being taxing or hard to position into impact. However, please apprehend that improving your awareness is not some aspect in an effort to display up in a single day, you want to be steady and everyday within the software of the strategies given underneath, for them to bear fruit.

What is attention?

In order to decorate some thing, you need to first have a clean facts of what it's miles. What is attention? In the handiest shape of explaining, it is not anything however the capacity to take your thoughts off multiple subjects and commit your complete awareness and interest to the singular task to hand.

What do you want to pay attention on?

As said earlier, it is very essential to decide and finalize the trouble on that you need to concentrate. The choice making detail have to be executed nicely. You can be confronted with numerous issues that require your hobby, however out of such troubles you need to prioritize and pick out out the only that is the most urgent.

Rule out the distractions

Now there are some people who can attention and art work in spite of having loud music gambling inside the information or with the television on, however for the giant majority of others who cannot reap this, it's miles very important to make sure that there are not any outdoor elements to distract you. The precept right proper here is to keep away from what is known as the "sensory overload". It has been confirmed in lots of researches that the common individual will pay interest better at the equal time as the amount of sensory inputs is minimum. And in case you can't get to a quiet area, learn how to near your thoughts towards the distraction.

Give it your whole

The key to wearing out popularity is to elevate the specific project within the the front of you to the maximum vital reputation, and thereby deliver it your whole. This experience of precedence that you attach to a few aspect will involuntarily help you concentrating better.

Don't panic, be calm

Concentration stems from a relaxed thoughts. Don't be jittery at the same time as face with a project. And this has greater to do with the mind of proper and lousy energy. When you live calm, awesome and present day energy flows thru you, whereas, while you panic, the distractive bad electricity deters you from being centered at the venture handy.

Time-outs

You also can have heard this countless instances earlier than, which you ought to take a ruin at regular periods to be more efficient. And allow's clearly reinstate that truth right here. It is simply real and holds appropriate in particular for human beings who've problem in concentrating. Medical research has proved it beyond doubt that the attention span of an average person does not exceed an hour and a half of at a stretch.

Take not unusual breaks, go out or walk to the window and take a breath of glowing air to rejuvenate your senses. Have a coffee or some light snack and bear in mind a few issue without a doubt unrelated to the paintings you have been doing prior to the damage. This is probably very critical, if you maintain questioning over the identical problem time and again all over again, even at some point of the harm time, the very idea of taking the smash is made redundant.

Energy drift

Learn to control the go with the go with the flow of electricity via your frame. The idea here is clean, as referred to in advance, immoderate wonderful strength allows you recognition and pay interest more while horrific electricity does the opposite to you. This glide of energy can be controlled through you to a big quantity. It does take masses of time to determine this out and grasp it, but it is with the aid of no way unimaginable. The key proper proper right here is to recognize what makes you enjoy excessive first-rate and content after which making sure that you are, in some way, in the presence of that issue while working. Similarly stay away from the variables that offer a feel of foreboding or make you revel in unhappy.

Meditation

We have saved the superb for the final. Meditation may be the fine tool that will help you focus higher and pay interest. Consider it as the maximum powerful weapon to your arsenal. Learn at the least a few meditation strategies and make sure which you exercise them daily for no tons much less than half of of an hour to 1 hour.

And while you do meditation, watch the breathing. Many half of of-baked theories endorse which you want to take aware attempt to govern your respiratory whilst meditating. But isn't always so, in truth, in location of controlling it, simply allow it is. Simply have a study the manner you are respiration. This helps you to cognizance as well.

The following five pointers will let you to discover ways to concentrate, regardless of what environment you are operating in:

F = Five More

There are special sorts of human beings – those who've learnt the manner to get round frustration and those who dearly choice that that they'd. This one is for you – in case you are halfway through doing something and you fell like throwing in the towel, do virtually 5 more.

Five more minutes, observe five more pages, cease 5 extra letters, some thing it is virtually do 5 extra in advance than you surrender and deliver in. This is a way used by many super people in a single-of-a-kind walks of existence. Athletes use it to push themselves beyond exhaustion element or through the pain barrier and you could use it to build up your interest and reputation via pushing beyond frustration.

Give it a glide – you'll discover that, when you get beyond a extraordinary element, your mind will kick into equipment yet again and your consciousness will come decrease returned.

O – One Think at a Time

"If I look burdened, it's because of the reality I'm thinking" – Samuel Goldwyn

Do you revel in as although you're completely disorganized and can't pay attention? Is it due to the fact your thoughts is usually on numerous different topics immediately, leaving you no room to consciousness on what truly desires to be completed? Use the Godfather plan to overcome it and make your thoughts a deal it surely can't refuse.

Believe it or now not, your mind can be bribed. When you inform yourself (or your thoughts) now not to fear about something, mainly if it isn't a high priority, you may robotically attention on it. Instead inform your mind to perform a little thing with a time restriction. For instance, you need to repay a credit score card debt and, to try this, you need to exercising what your disposable earnings is. Tell your mind that you will do it this night while you get domestic however, for the following half-hour, you want to pay interest on a presentation you have become equipped for a excessive-powered customer. That need to smooth your thoughts and could will let you cognizance on what's critical.

If you could't smooth your thoughts, write the whole lot down on a to-do listing. That manner, you may locate you neglect approximately them till you come back against them in your listing. A to-do list approach that you aren't having to use up your brain as a highbrow to-do list, as a give up end result liberating it up for larger and higher subjects.

C – Conquer Procrastination

Procrastinators are individuals who dispose of doing something mainly subjects that should be achieved in a timely manner. Next time you feel like getting rid of doing some thing, ask your self three questions:

•Do I in reality ought to do that activity?

•Should I get it finished so it isn't continuously playing on my thoughts?

•Will the procedure be any less tough if I leave it to later?

Asking your self those questions can push your mind into specializing in a selected undertaking due to the fact they make you sincerely consider the assignment. They make you resist the reality that it isn't going away and that placing it off continuously will virtually make you enjoy extra responsible; with the intention to cause the challenge taking up hundreds extra of a while than is important.

U = Use your arms as a shape of blinkers

Imagine your thoughts is a camera and that your eyes are the aperture. Most of the time, your eyes take in what's happening and your thoughts is appearing as a kind of splendid-mindset awareness. We are in reality capable of considering numerous topics right now and however operating effectively.

So, permit's bear in mind that you want to replace your thoughts to telephoto attention. You want to focus a hundred% of your attention on one detail to get it completed, say, a hard letter which you want to write down. Cup your arms across the additives of your eyes, consequently blocking off out the entirety round you – in effect, they will be out of sight, for that reason they will be from your thoughts. Cupping your hand round your eyes focuses your attention on one issue at a time and you could honestly teach your mind on this manner.

It's called classical conditioning and it have turn out to be first found inside the 1890's with the beneficial useful resource of Pavlov, a Russian psychologist. He placed that his puppies salivated when they have been fed and in the end commenced out to salivate each time he walked into a room – because of the fact they associated him with meals. He achieved an take a look at in which he rang a bell and gave his canine food on the equal time. After some of times repeating this, the puppies would possibly salivate really at the sound of the bell. In the equal way, thru cupping your hands spherical your eyes and repeating it you may teach your mind into studying that this makes you interest and supply interest to the assignment available.

S = Seeing as though it is for the number one or the final time

Have you ever heard the saying, "in the right proper right here and now"? How often are you able to really say that you are present mentally? By that I advise that, extra regularly than now not, at the equal time as you are, permit's say sitting at your desk, your thoughts is extra than in all likelihood some different location. Next time you find out your mind wandering a long way from you are and what you're doing, take an extraordinary go searching you and open your eyes to what you note. Study your environment, honestly see it and address it and your mind will snap again to hobby.

Chapter 2: Mental Exercises to Boost Concentration

As with all unique styles of wearing occasions, highbrow bodily sports can be very monotonous. They require you to patiently stay with the everyday and persevere. But after you do, the results may be magnificent. When it involves bodily games, our mind, or to be extra particular, our mind is just like, our limbs. You exercise session your hands regularly and that they become increasingly more robust. Similarly, the ones intellectual physical games can make your thoughts sharper and the extent of focus shall float up. Listed herein below are some of the only mind physical sports for you. But first....

Think of Your Mind as a Muscle

This is important as regards to strengthening up your recognition and interest. You mind is an "hobby" muscle in a whole lot the same manner as you have got physical muscle companies within the relaxation of your body. Both styles of muscle are restricted in the quantity of energy they've at a given time − if they're used frequently, they'll make more potent up, f no longer used frequently, they'll atrophy and, even as they'll be used, they need rest and restoration afterwards.

Just before you begin a top notch exercising on the gymnasium, you could get a sense of doubt that you could virtually do it. The identical goes to your mind when you are about to cope with a tough piece of labor. You ought to set your mind to the system and buckle down to doing it.

Your mind will probable begin to wander halfway thru the artwork a few factor else will seize your interest probably, a few factor that looks lots more thrilling and, nine times out of ten, you may permit yourself to be distracted. But, if you inform your self that you want to get on, you have dig in deeper, you'll be surprised at clearly how a good buy more your thoughts has to provide.

The following bodily sports are designed as a form of brain exercise to bolster up your hobby. Let's face it, you won't building up muscle power via sitting round all day and also you in reality received't constructing up intellectual strength if you limit your consciousness. Your mind dreams exercise and it goals resistive exercise in a bargain the same manner as your frame goals resistive workout. Your mind wishes to be challenged as a way to stretch it and, within the method, your mind muscle will expand cognizance fibers. These carrying sports are designed to boom your interest so you are capable of take on heavier intellectual limits:

Increase your awareness gradually

You don't throw your self proper right into a heavy physical education software program with out constructing up to it and the identical is going for your mind. You need to regularly boom the strength of your thoughts muscle in order that it could take on greater. This is in which the "pomodoro" method comes into play. This is a method in which you set your self a timer, say for forty five minutes, and you determine till the timer goes off. Then you can take a 15 minute harm. But, in case your consciousness isn't as much as scratch, you don't want to be diving without delay into it. So, set your self a five minute timer. Focus absolutely for your paintings for the ones 5 minutes after which have a 2 minute damage. Do each other 5 mins, observed thru every one of a kind 2 minute break. Each day, add some other five mins to the timer and a few unique 2 minutes to your damage. By the time 9 days is up, you want to be targeted enough to art work for that 45 mins with out preventing, before worthwhile your self with an 18 minute destroy. Once you get settled in to that routine, you can paintings on lengthening the time you parent and lowering the time of your breaks - but not to the quantity wherein they disappear altogether.

Write a to-do list on your distractions

The net is a wonderful aspect however, due to the fact we can find out pretty much some detail we need on it, we will be inclined to appearance a few element up the minute we take into account it. Consequently, our reputation and attention is drawn away from what we're doing. That may moreover sound adequate, due to the reality you only want to test the climate, it'll best take 2 mins, proper? Wrong. Not quality do you run the run the hazard of being tempted to truely test your Facebook page or your email whilst you are on line, it also takes, on not unusual, 25 minutes to get decrease decrease lower back into your art work. Plus, the fact that your attention is shifting from side to side surely does drain your thoughts of its power.

So, whilst you take into account a few element you'll possibly want to check on the net, right it down on a piece of paper and push it to at least one element till you are on a harm otherwise you get domestic.

Build up your self-control

Willpower is a top notch issue – while you've were given it. It lets in you to dismiss those distractions, to push on along side your project until it's completed and now not get sidetracked in any respect. Strengthening your strength of mind takes time however the great manner to do it's miles to cope with huge desires and use the pomodoro method we stated in advance, frequently building up the time you spend on that cause. Another technique that has been set up to art work is to switch fingers. If you're right-exceeded person, transfer to the use of your left hand for a while and vice versa.

Practice being aware all day

You should get into the addiction of dedicating among 10 and 20 minutes of every day to meditation, as a way of clearing your thoughts and taking off it up for the day earlier or closing it down after paintings. On pinnacle of that, workout being aware all day as properly. All this is, is concentrating your complete hobby on one challenge at a time, slowing down and considering all the feelings you experience on the identical time as you're doing that assignment – physical and mentally. This will work to enhance your attention span for those times at the same time as it's miles honestly wanted and it will let you to push away unwanted distractions.

Exercise your body

Physical exercising has been shown to have a useful effect on intellectual power and fitness. People who get worried in mild workout earlier than they take a take a look at or buckle right down to a assignment have an lousy lot higher interest spans than folks that don't. This is because of the truth exercising boosts your thoughts's capability to disregard any distractions and will increase your strength of will as well.

Take a while studying

With such plenty of people the use of capsules, smartphones and e-readers in recent times, it's created a culture of human beings now not completing what they start. Let me offer an explanation for that – a trendy research showed that simplest round five% of folks who begin reading a chunk of writing or a ebook on this type of devices will in no way finish it. And 38% will in no way get beyond the first couple of paragraphs. So, the fact that research display, with these sorts of digital gadgets, reading has lengthy lengthy past up with the useful resource of 40%, approach not some thing. In actual phrases, there is a great deal less reading occurring and greater scrolling through pages instead.

That' a actual disgrace due to the truth analyzing lengthy articles or books can in reality red meat up the mind. Long articles may not robotically advocate that they may be higher, from time to time there may be a outstanding deal of records, complex records that have to be stretched over an prolonged article or a ebook. To skip some aspect because it appears too lengthy is a particular no-no and might bring about you missing out on a ton of beneficial statistics and thoughts stretching as well. Pick up a ebook this night time time and in reality try to get into it – it's going to do you the power of wonderful.

As well as that, attempt to discover the time to have a take a look at or 3 prolonged informative articles per week. They will really expand your thoughts, and also you'll be amazed at what you can examine along the manner as well!

Be curious – continuously

The greater curiosity you have approximately the area and about matters round you, the higher your hobby may be. Try this little take a look at to test out how being curious approximately a few aspect could make your capability to attention on it final longer:

•Draw a dot on a bit of paper and positioned it within the the front of you or pin it to a wall. Now interest on it. One of topics will take region – your discipline of imaginative and prescient will blur so that you will not without a doubt see some issue or you may discover yourself searching at some factor however the dot. However, ask your self a few questions on the dot – how huge is it, what form, what shade, and so forth., at the equal time as you are looking at it, successive questions to your mind and you may find out which you provide hobby to it for plenty longer.

Charles Darwin modified into taken into consideration one of the most vital masters of this – he should spend all day simply gazing flora, vegetation or animals. He had a interest approximately things that never dies and, by using way of the usage of looking at a few thing for hours, he ought to have a look at more and more about it, truly with the useful useful resource of asking himself questions about it and via looking at it from high-quality angles and views.

Practice attentive listening

Focus isn't pretty a good deal your running conduct, it's additionally an crucial life potential. To be able to listen your interest on circle of relatives or pals with out your mind wandering is a useful potential to research and, even as you're focusing, you're strengthening up your thoughts muscle tissue. When you are speakme with humans in destiny, workout truely taking note of them, focusing all your interest on them and no longer for your cellphone or the sport at the TV.

In a brief at the same time as, we're going to examine a few interest carrying activities which you need to make a point of training. In order to get the most out of those, take a look at these suggestions:

•Find somewhere quiet wherein you'll be with the aid of yourself and no longer be disturbed.

•Be cushty – maximum human beings discover it less complicated to take a seat down on a chair or you may sit down move-legged on the floor. You need to sit collectively with your spine erect despite the fact that

•Take a few deep calm breaths and loosen up your complete body, little by little, via pointing your direction to every muscle in turn, starting out of your toes and running up for your head

•Practice all of the physical games for 10 minutes initially. After some weeks you can start growing the time to fifteen mins and so on

•Do the carrying occasions inside the order they will be listed in.

•Start with the number one exercising and practice it each unmarried day till you may do it with out being distracted and without your thoughts wandering some location else for as a minimum 3 minutes constantly

•If you do get distracted, start yet again until the ten minutes has surpassed

•Be very honest with your self – simplest circulate directly to exercise while you are happy that you have mastered the primary one nicely and function practiced it with out being distracted

•Do no longer set yourself a timetable as this can actually grow to be anxious you. If you positioned your self a mission of jogging toward a specific workout for, permit's say five days. Two matters are likely to take vicinity – first you may be disillusioned if you could't hold close it within the ones five days and second, you may circulate at once to the subsequent exercise in advance than you already to.

•Remember that reading the ones sporting sports can take days, every now and then weeks or months

•Focus your whole interest on the carrying sports and do no longer allow your self to reflect onconsideration on anything else. Make exquisite you do no longer nod off or burst off right into a daydream. If you do locate your thoughts wandering onto something else, stop and begin once more. Once you're proficient, preserve on with the same exercise but for an extended time and try to do training in someday

•Never do an excessive amount of to begin with and actually do no longer attempt to do all the carrying sports right now. Take it smooth and don't overdo it

•Don't be disheartened if you do locate it difficult to pay interest or are without problems distracted. Nobody gets it first time around; all you want to do is persevere and in no way, ever surrender. Remember this — even those who've effective attention capabilities needed to begin on the start and discover ways to workout their minds as nicely.

It in reality doesn't depend when you have a low stage of attention and attention first of all. Just like your frame, whilst you go to the gym, your mind muscle businesses can be exercised and strengthened as nicely — it honestly takes attempt and training.

Given time, you may discover that your interest abilities are tons better, that you will be able to attention for your given duties and can be capable of pay attention, irrespective of in that you're. Even in activities which might be attempting, you may be able to popularity and pay hobby your thinking on the identical time as staying calm and accumulated further to absolutely snug.

To get the complete benefit of those physical sports you need to practice every one for a similarly week at the same time as you experience you have mastered it:

Count the terms

This is one of the most effective thoughts sporting activities ever. Take the newspaper, pick out a piece of writing and begin counting the quantity of phrase within the first paragraph of the factor. Redo it another time to ensure the determine is accurate. Go on to the following paragraph. In this style, cover the whole net page. You can also use a ebook or mag for that reason. There is handiest problem that you need to make certain; do not rely in conjunction with your arms. The complete exercise want to be finished with the eyes by myself.

Count backwards

This one may additionally sound clean, however only deceptively so. In your mind, with out pronouncing the numbers out aloud, begin counting backwards. Easy? Then try this, begin counting over again from 100, but bypass the 4 digits in amongst, as an instance a hundred, 96, ninety two and so forth.

Fruity technique

Sit down on a chair, pick out a fruit of your desire, and keep it out for your palm. Now virtually supply hobby to the fruit. Run your eyes over it, consider its fragrance, visualize to your thoughts its taste, the feel, the feeling of biting into it and so forth. Do no longer reflect onconsideration on the ancillary subjects much like the price, the shop from which you got it and so forth. The concept is to dam out every one in all a kind concept out of your thoughts and recall the fruit on the most fundamental diploma.

Glass of water

Take a medium sized glass of water and sit down down on a chair. Extend an arm outwards and vicinity the glass on the outstretched palm. Any tremors or shaking shall be seen with the useful resource of the ripples at the ground of the water. Now pay interest difficult by means of the use of searching at the glass. When you do this, your hands will ordinary themselves. Shift the glass into the opportunity hand and repeat the gadget.

Look however don't anticipate

This is a mild variant of the "Fruity technique" given above. In this example, pick up a small item collectively with pen, pencil or paper clip and check it, concentrating hard. But do no longer reflect onconsideration on it. Just maintain searching at the object with out questioning some thing approximately it. It may be a bit hard within the starting, but you'll decorate with time. Keep doing again and again and it's going to artwork wonders to the quantity of popularity.

To colour or now not

This exercising is on a better stage and will exercising handiest when you have mastered the ones given above. What you have to do right right here is, draw a geometrical figure on a sheet of paper. It may be circle, triangle or rectangle. But something it is, ensure it's miles small and now not overtly big. Now fill the indoors of the discern with a tremendous and contrasting coloration which incorporates red or yellow or black.

Then comes the hard element, have a take a look at the picture inside the the front of you and visualize the discern by myself. Ignore the shade, forget approximately approximately your surroundings and actually block out any mind out of your mind. Simply take a look at the paper and imaging the decide or outline of the picture. The Chair workout

Okay, now right here it's far, simply sit. That's all there can be, just choose out a immediately returned, comfortable chair and sit. Well a bit extra genuinely, ensure that at the same time as sitting, you aren't moving a muscle. Your frame shouldn't circulate a millimeter besides your chest and nostrils, for breathing. This may also moreover moreover sound accessible to you, however it is in reality a hard one. You might not be capable of do it for added than five minutes at a stretch, but exercising tough and join a cause of fifteen mins. It is a type of compound exercising due to the fact if carried out well, it may lighten up your entire body.

Breathing outside and inside

You may also moreover already recognize of this but its effectiveness warrants it a place in any listing of intellectual sporting sports to beautify attention. Sit upright on a chair or at the ground, together collectively along with your head and decrease lower back in a proper away line. Press your index finger toward your proper nostril and breathe in lightly thru your left, mentally ticking off ten seconds. Now remove your finger and exhale through your right nose, yet again taking ten seconds to accomplish that. Now repeat the complete method with the opportunity finger and left nose. This exercise ought to be finished at the least 20 instances at a stretch.

Noise cancellation

Noise is considered one of the maximum critical motives why we cannot pay interest and recognition well. So allow us to tackle it head on. The best region to do this will be on a park subsequent to the street. Close your eyes and take a stock of all the sounds round you. Now, pick out a legitimate and attention on it, blocking out the whole lot else. After or 3 mins, switch your recognition to some different sound and recognition on it, ignoring everything else in turn.

Blank out

We have saved the most difficult one for the final. Intentionally easy yourself out. Do not reflect onconsideration on a few issue for a minute. Completely block out the whole lot out of your thoughts. This might also show to be extraordinarily tough in the beginning, however do not give up. Keep strolling on it and often boom the term to 5 mins and from there to 10 and so forth. There is most effective one principle to this workout, your thoughts should be certainly loose, and now not even a unmarried concept need to invade your mind. The time of the day, in which you are, what you are doing, what you need to do and many others. Are all mind that have a tendency to barge into our mind whilst we try to smooth out. But face up to such mind via way of the usage of gaining mastery over your idea method.

Chapter 3: Tips for Better Concentration

Now that we've got had been given protected the various techniques and strategies for enhancing attention and awareness, it is time to provide the very last contact. Once you're nicely versed with the intellectual physical video video games, you could keep the ones pointers in thoughts to spherical it off nicely.

Push through frustration

This is all approximately pushing your limits. When you feel saturated and anticipate which you cannot preserve your degree of hobby for another minute, persuade your self to provide in five more minutes. Force yourself to have a take a look at a couple of more pages. Tackle greater issues and so on.

Right at the same time as the temptation to surrender hits you, push for a few different 5 minutes. Those 5 mins remember wide variety loads. This is corresponding to athletes and bodybuilders who educate to move beyond the component of exhaustion and growth their electricity and stamina. Similarly, push your thoughts and heighten the attention stages.

Prioritize

Prioritize your responsibilities. If faced with a couple of issues, make a highbrow listing and take within the hassle that ranks the very great and leave the relaxation for the instant. For this you have had been given to research the specific problems and plan the execution. And at the same time as doing the project at hand, do not worry about those which you have stored aside. Just interest at the artwork available and deliver attention to that on my own.

Tunnel imaginative and prescient

You are studying a e-book and find that past a factor, you can't pay attention? Here is a short tip, cup your face along facet your fingers in this shape of manner that your imaginative and prescient is constrained to just the e-book alone. Create a sort of tunnel vision in which you cannot see anything apart from the page you are studying. This helps in focusing at the assignment on hand higher, as this brings into your belief manner beneath your command.

The first and final look

This tip comes in handy when you have to concentrate while looking at figures or patterns. Confront the pattern or determine as though it's miles the number one and last time you may be searching at it. Create this experience of self urgency and your consciousness will involuntarily bypass up in studying that truth. It is the regular human tendency to procrastinate and do away with tough topics for later. This body of thoughts isn't conducive in enhancing your ranges of popularity, even if you need to.

Decide what's outstanding for you

Throughout the final 3 chapters we have indexed out various strategies and strategies for improving your hobby and numerous tips for use in conjecture with them. Do now not doubt, even for a second the efficacy of the strategies, however you want to apprehend the easy truth that not every body is alike and a way which may additionally additionally show to paintings for one won't be fruitful for the opportunity.

And this is precisely the purpose why we reckoned we have to upload this little tip - decide what is extremely good for you. The human thoughts is an enigma, the intricacies of which have in no way been clearly understood in its entirety. Hence in choice to going via the textbook, strive out and take a look at the exclusive techniques and techniques that have been stated and described herein and verify which is going for you the satisfactory.

10 Tips Specifically for Concentration at Work

You may think which you are organized due to the truth you preserve a time table and you write a to-do lists however are these simply helping you to get more finished or is all of your recognition being taken up through using certainly completing those in choice to for your art work? Organization is one of the more crucial matters but, for it to artwork efficiently, you need as a manner to focus. You need an amazing way to sit down down and recognition cautiously to your duties for more than one hours or more — consider it or now not, even focusing for half of an hour can bring about greater being finished that in case you ship all day preventing off distractions and seeking to do several topics right away.

The following tips are designed that will help you get your self into a rustic of attention in the administrative center:

Cut the noise out

While that the noise round you is a severe distraction, do you without a doubt do something positive about decreasing it out? Yes, it could be tempting to have your electronic mail symptoms switched on, your immediate messaging activated and your smartphone on but you don't need to deal with they all whenever they ping to existence. Turn them off, at the least at the equal time as you are attempting to pay attention and simplest placed them on while you're on a wreck. It can take spherical 15 – 25 mins a terrific manner to clearly get into a real us of a of cognizance and if you are being distracted each brief time thru using an email coming in, your mum texting you or your mate stoning up on IM then you definately definately cannot likely get yourself into that kingdom of hobby. Stick to answering your emails simplest at set times and ask that humans don't touch you except it is an emergency and request aht you aren't disturbed. If a part of your interest is to answer the phones and notice to clients while they come in, time desk huge responsibilities for while things aren't so busy.

Structure your surroundings

Where you're operating has a big effect on the way you recognition on your paintings. Try and characteristic your self so you are going thru distractions, which include windows or doorways, even the cellular phone. That way, you and look up to assess any sound that could in reality destroy your distraction and then positioned it from your thoughts. If you have got your again to the door and a person is available in, you may routinely look up and far from your art work and your interest is damaged.

Know your desires

Before you begin paintings, make a list of your dreams so you are easy on exactly what is predicted. If you don't you will really get forced and as a manner to make cognizance now not feasible.

Divide a venture into blobs

Big jobs can every now and then appearance daunting so smash massive obligations down into smaller one, making every one a machine of its personal. For each one, without a doubt discover the desires and the course you could take to get running on it. Each blob, or phase, ought to be truly related to the others in a proper series so ensure you recommend the complete way out in steps, in a logical manner

Know the venture tips

Be easy at the guidelines for the mission you may tackle. What elegant of extremely good is needed? Are there any constraints which you need to be aware about? How prolonged does it want to be, what fashion need to it be written in? If your guidelines are bendy then mark out how you are going to finish the gadget in advance than you start. That way, you'll not locate your self dropping consciousness as you try to schooling session what wants to be accomplished.

Have a cut-off date

Deadlines can be powerful as well as a problem while you are attempting to pay hobby. Deadlines have to make it very smooth to overlook about things that aren't critical and that will help you accelerate. Give your self a tough and rapid time for each part of the technique; that way you could locate it lots less complicated and you received't maintain messing round looking for to make it complex or over-extravagant.

Deadlines turn out to be disadvantageous while you start disturbing approximately how a whole lot – or little – time you have got were given got left in desire to focusing on the task itself. Use a ultimate date at the same time as:

•You have handiest a constrained amount of time to complete the undertaking in. Split the challenge into particular closing dates and eliminate any nonessential art work

•If you observed you are dropping sight of the big photo, I.E., it's easy to increase what you're doing to healthy in new mind and you run the threat of going manner over aim. Deadlines will assist hold a modicum of manage.

•If you're a procrastinator! Tight closing dates save you you form now not doing the art work and from disturbing about getting it finished

Use cut-off dates as it should be – putting one for every activity will only serve to get you compelled out and if you want to cause your attention to shift.

Get spherical the roadblocks

Roadblocks arise at the same time as you run out of mind in any other case you find out your recognition wavering. Get round those thru making plans subjects out on paper or brainstorming it, each with yourself paintings with a colleague. Writing topics down can assist preserve your cognizance in test.

Isolate your self

Stay far from humans in case you actually need to get your paintings achieved. Unless you want them to finish your paintings, they'll handiest serve to distract you. Set aside a hard and speedy time in which you can close your self away in an empty place of work to artwork. If you may't do that, located a be part of up asking human beings to depart you on my own until a tough and speedy time and divert your phone someplace else.

Be healthful

You already apprehend that a healthy body equals a sharp thoughts. What you eat and drink has an impact at the way you observed and concentrate, Make sure you get lots of sleep, don't use stimulants in conjunction with caffeine, don't eat too any fatty ingredients. Just strive reducing out one terrible dependancy for one month and note what the impact on your attention ranges is.

Be affected individual

Sit and think about your paintings for severa mins earlier than you without a doubt start. You will revel in an urge to upward thrust up and pass do some thing else however, if you take a seat down patiently, that urge will pass, and your workflow will come truely. You can be able to in reality expect out your artwork and go along with that go with the flow.

Chapter 4: Methods for Improving Learning Capacity

In this monetary disaster we can have a look at some of the satisfactory techniques for reinforcing your mastering functionality. These are a hard and fast of recommendations that take a healthful method in place of being fixated on any singular concept or method. Before we move into those, permit's take a better take a look at a way to enhance your memory, one of the maximum essential components about analyzing.

Improving your memory isn't as hard as you may think. The biggest trouble is overcoming the concept that reminiscence is static, that it doesn't alternate. It does and it could be stepped forward in a good buy the same way as you'll beautify any talent – thru exercise.

We all realize that there are kinds of memory – short and prolonged-time period. We use our quick-term reminiscence to maintain portions of statistics that we might need right away, like a call. According to investigate, quick-term memory is able to maintaining directly to approximately 7 portions of data and, as soon as it's whole, some thing has to drop off.

Long-time period memory is to maintain information that we don't want to recognize right away. When you look at for checks, that's wherein the facts goes, into your prolonged-term memory. Memorable activities are saved there too.

So, how do you decorate your reminiscence?

Your memory lives to your thoughts

You may expect that I am putting forward the apparent proper right here but now not each person realizes that reminiscence is fashioned inside the mind. So, it have to bypass with out announcing that, if some thing improves the health of your brain, it robotically improves your memory. Two strategies which is probably demonstrated to keep the mind stimulated are physical exercise an sports that stimulate the mind, together with crossword puzzles or Sudoku puzzles.

But, there's some element else that permits particularly and that is maintaining your frame healthful. Watching what you consume and ruling stress from your existence are critical factors in helping your mind to recognition nicely. Getting sufficient sleep is vital and, it ought to be stated, taking vitamin and herbal nutritional dietary supplements do no longer have the identical impact on your frame as getting the identical nutrients via a healthful food regimen, so ingesting well is the number one component you need to interest on.

How to Improve your Memory

The following suggestions will will can help you discover ways to attention your interest and listen:

• Focus on what you are doing. Multitasking may be the in buzzword of the day but, spending an excessive amount of time on juggling multiple duties should have one end result – you could no longer attention at the assignment accessible. Your thoughts wishes with the intention to take inside the statistics you are studying and it desires time to do that. If you are continuously flicking your consciousness among a couple of responsibilities, that isn't always going to take location. Stop multitasking, begin focusing.

• Smell, flavor, contact, hear and notice it. Use your senses, all of them, whilst you need to encode information into your reminiscence. The greater senses you use, the much less tough it's miles going to be to ingrain a few component in your memory. If you want to remember a name, look the individual in the eye while you are meeting them for the primary time and repeat their call, shake their hand. You have now used 4 out of the five senses and you can remember their call lots much less hard.

• Repeat things to yourself. Repetition works; the extra you repeat some factor the much more likely you're to consider it. Don't do it constantly notwithstanding the fact that, repeat the records you want to recall over a spaced out time body

• Put prolonged statistics into chunks. Think about a ten-digit telephone large range. Despite the fact that our short-term reminiscence can awesome preserve 7 portions of information, you can bear in mind the ones 10 digits, due to the fact you harm them into chunks. Instead of seeing 10 separate numbers you be aware it as a couple of quantities of facts – area ode, prefix and range. You can do this with any facts – virtually divide a large quantity into smaller chunks and focus on memorizing each separate chunk.

• Organize records that you want to memorize. Brains like commercial enterprise organization and, in a fantastic deal the equal manner as a e-book is damaged into chapters, you may wreck down your statistics.

• Use mnemonics. These gadgets will let you to bear in mind complicated data by way of the use of the usage of using acronyms, imagery, songs or rhyme. Think about a scientific scholar – they may often memorize bones and symptoms and signs and symptoms and signs and symptoms and signs and symptoms of illnesses through springing up with sentences wherein the primary letter of each word will correspond to a selected symptom or bones. Think approximately this one, some thing we have been all taught at college — the manner to take into account the colors of the rainbow:

- Richard

- Of

- York

- Gave

- Battle

- In

- Vain

The first letter of every word is the number one letter of the corresponding shade and the order they skip within the rainbow — red, orange, yellow, green, blue, indigo, violet. That's how easy it's miles

• Find your personal way of mastering. There isn't a "one length suits all" mentality almost approximately analyzing, truely all and sundry is extremely good. Find the style that works for you, although it's an extended manner really tremendous from the manner every body else learns. Some people analyze thru writing things down, others studies via recording a session and a few people examine via doing in preference to listening.

• Connect the dots. Try to observe establishments, that way you are probably to maintain in thoughts topics plenty much less hard. When you first soak up a piece of facts, take into account the manner it relates to some thing – you could have extra danger of remembering each subjects that manner. Connect the dots among new facts and the records this is already for your thoughts.

As we broaden antique, we will be predisposed to count on that our reminiscence definitely receives worse. It doesn't must even though. By following the above pointers, you could preserve the edge in your memory for so long as you want to.

Now, onto those hints we talked about on the begin of this bankruptcy:

Don't prevent studying

The awesome way to enhance your studying potential is to genuinely keep getting to know more. It has been proved in countless researches thru scientists that the extra you stimulate the thoughts thru studying, the extra might be your capacity to research further. This capacity of the human thoughts to imbibe extra while it's far continuously inspired is called "pruning". Moreover this can boom your retention ability as nicely.

The handiest example of this phenomenon is studying a ultra-modern language. Learn a few key terms and prevent there and you may in no way master the language. However keep gaining information of new terms and terms every day and in a few unspecified time within the destiny it'll no longer just be your knowledge over the language in case you want to enhance but furthermore the quantum of new subjects that you could examine.

Multi-pronged method

This is the tried and tested approach of using more than one strategies to test the same element. For example, to investigate a concept, read it, write what you have got take a look at on a paper, be privy to a recording of the concept and visualize it. Each technique includes a special location of the mind. The precept is to clearly incorporate the maximum range of areas simply so, all taken together a entire photo can be created. This method ensures that you have in fact discovered out a concept rather of actually mugging it up.

Take up teaching

It is time honored concept that, the best way to study a few component and to ensure that it remains to your head is to educate it to a person. The whole way of teaching involves walking your personal memory and reproducing what you have got got were given saved there. When you give an explanation for a concept to any other person, your thoughts has to accumulate up all of the free snippets and bind them collectively into a fixed of coherent information. This also consists of translating the facts into verbal records which once more cements your knowledge.

Relate and feature a take a look at

This is a way this is incredibly effective in studying hard and novel thoughts. Relate the fact to absolutely precise and unrelated matters along with a image or a difficult and speedy of numerals or a piece of music or a jingle. When you accomplish that, your mind stores the truth at the side of the related consider. This differentiates the precise idea shape different comparable ones that you could have determined in advance.

This technique is specifically beneficial in getting to know scientific requirements that adjust from every different in very minute factors.

Hands on method

There is big amount of distinction amongst reading something, retaining it in a part of your mind and in reality placing that located out knowledge into exercise. When you obtain this, it in reality solidifies that concept in your mind. Practice what you have were given discovered out on a ordinary foundation and you switch out to be thorough in that and it frees up "place" for your thoughts to look at greater. Let us take the earlier given instance of studying a contemporary language. Just going to schooling will quality train you the theoretical factors of the language. But on the equal time, if you watch movies within the language and speak with nearby audio device of the language, it permits you obtain an entire new degree of mastery over it.

Refer in choice to remember

There is a big misconception that if you have learned something and while you try to reproduce it or say it aloud, you have to not searching for advice from the source cloth, if you can not retrieve it from memory. This isn't always actual, haven't any qualms in starting the ebook and referring. A cursory look is all that it may take on the way to surely bring it out. This furthermore improves your retention functionality and permits you examine extra.

Test your self

Test your self frequently on what you've got were given discovered out within the past. Take a aware try to step from your consolation zone and problem your self to self-exam in your records. This no longer pleasant improves your readability on the thoughts, but moreover will boom your recalling capacity. Frequent checks also make you extra cushty with reproducing on name for what you have discovered.

Say no to multitasking

Generally, the capability to multitask is appeared as a few thing to be reputable. But present day studies studies have shown that multitasking may additionally have unfavourable effects in your capacity to have a have a look at in addition. Instead of hopping among obligations, take one after the other, repair a intention time and cease it with utmost interest. This manner your readability on the problem may be better, the concept will live in your mind for an extended duration and your efficiency in reproducing it on a later day can also be better.

Chapter 5: Various Techniques to Improve Your Learning

In this financial disaster, let us have a look at the various techniques you may nonetheless rent to enhancing their learning competencies.

Elaborative Interrogation

Under this approach, we question the cause within the again of something in desire to query what it is all approximately. In other terms, the query that one asks under this technique is why and no longer what. For instance, even as you are given a precept to study, in place of clearly analyzing the concept again and again to memorize the postulates of it, you can begin thinking why the precept turned into formulated inside the first place.

This way, the best judgment stays in your thoughts for an prolonged time thereby making it less difficult on the manner to apprehend the idea in totality. However, it could not be as smooth because it sounds at the same time as you really placed the approach into exercise. Prior understanding of the scenario is every so often required to even recognize the answer behind the "why" question. Keeping that apart, it's miles an effective way analyzing technique. It can produce awesome consequences with a few exercise.

Distributed workout

This approach addresses the problem of retention of information studied over an prolonged time period. We often must do not forget topics that we studied inside the beginning of an academic twelve months within the direction of the final tests. How is it feasible for the thoughts to remember some element you studied nearly a 365 days lower back completely?

Instead of analyzing all of it in haste at some degree within the week in advance than the final checks, what one should do is take a look at the issue each month. This manner, it need to no longer be a trouble while you're making geared up for the final assessments. The longer you preference to take into account subjects, the extra even need to be the space amongst reading lessons of the worried subject be counted. Distributed exercise helps in increasing the memory power and longer retention prices.

Self-Explanation

Often we genuinely have a look at subjects and expect to recollect it after sooner or later. When we attempt to do not forget stuff and deliver an cause in the back of ourselves the concept, we find it difficult. This is due to the reality we push off the motive aspect to a later time. Under this technique, the reason follows the studying consultation proper away. We regularly apprehend subjects while we try to provide an motive of it to ourselves out loud.

For example, you have been suffering to take a look at an essential occasion related to the Civil conflict. What you can do after analyzing the passage is, offer an reason in the back of the chain of events to your self loudly. This manner, you'll be capable of apprehend and examine the difficulty short. Also, it is simpler to mark out the regions wherein you are not smooth on the equal time as you try explaining your self. Otherwise, it would prima facie look like you understood the whole thing. You might be in for a impolite surprise later while the textual content you had examine a few days another time appears clearly alien to you. Summarizing

Under this method, all one has to do is have a look at a passage, summarize it in few quick lines. This exercising reflects how masses one has understood the passage. It isn't feasible to summarize a text with out understanding what it's far about. This is probably one of the reasons why a few professors insist on the scholars taking notes for the duration of a lecture.

When one summarizes a passage or a lecture of their very personal terms, they might be capable of hold in mind it properly the following time they have a look at their notes. Writing notes have a few other advantage. You is probably in a role to brush up the entire difficulty rely in a rely of minutes with the useful resource of clearly searching at your notes alternatively of having to go through the whole text over again.

Highlighting and underlining

This method ought to become quite redundant if not achieved carefully. Under this method, the critical factors or terms are highlighted or underlined for easy reference. Now it is not less complicated to determine out the crucial element factors in a passage besides you take a look at it with utmost awareness and apprehend it. However, this may be the downside of this technique as nicely. Students regularly might also additionally sincerely spotlight random sentences and the whole tool will become futile. If applied properly, highlighting handiest important sentences will assist in revising the passage over again.

Creating Mock Tests

We regularly have a look at tests and checks as a few difficulty scary. We fail to recognize that the concern for those assessments might be springing up from loss of sufficient data approximately the mission. How to triumph over this worry? Well, ask a chum to set you some mock query papers so you can write. When you supply those mock assessments, you will be in a better role to analyze how masses you have without a doubt learnt and understood. You can reread the quantities you probable did not answer properly inside the mock query paper. This way, you could don't forget the solution all the time.

Making up Key Words

Sometimes we do not forget stuff on the equal time as it's miles associated with fun. Why now not make gaining knowledge of a fun exercise as properly? Learn to partner key terms with any critical concept to apprehend in addition to recall it. Mnemonics (we mentioned it in advance) assist you to memorize a passage better. Still don't get the drift of it? Remember the manner we have been taught the 9 planets while we were kids?

"My Very Elegant Mother Just Showed Us Nine Planets" – the starting letter of each phrase in this phrase represents a planet.

So the concept is to discover key terms associated with the passage and use it to have a have a look at. This manner gaining knowledge of will become amusing, progressive and smooth.

Associating Images

Have you questioned as to why we bear in mind a story we examine eons inside the beyond better than a passage we read the day earlier than? Well, the solution is straightforward. When we study or take note of a story, we picture it inner our heads. That is the motive why we vividly keep in mind the tale even after a long time. When we strive extending this principle to analyzing different things, the results need to surely artwork to your prefer.

You have problem remembering a physics take a look at? Try visualizing the entire device inner your head as you take a look at it. That manner, the photograph stays to your thoughts longer than you may keep in mind. It is a good deal less difficult to retrieve the picture out of your memory as opposed to the whole text. This may additionally even enhance your memory electricity.

Rereading

Rereading is one of the great studying techniques. The difference between studying and rereading is from time to time the distinction among listening to and listening. We often observe some issue without certainly specializing in it. When you reread it, it makes more experience and remains internal your head. Whenever you have a look at some aspect for the primary time, make certain you reread it at once that allows you to ensure which you have understood it genuinely. This can also assist you undergo in mind subjects with out issues due to the truth your mind is processing some component all over again.

Interleaved Practice

Sometimes, studying all the topics under a unmarried unit might be monotonous and dull. The tempo of reading can even come down as quickly as monotony devices in. How to cope with it? Interleaving does no longer consciousness on analyzing subjects in whole blocks. It as an possibility focuses on studying troubles in a haphazard fashion. However, if hired loosely, this technique ought to possibly truly backfire on the man or woman.

Chapter 6: The Science inside the again of Concentration

Do you ever find out yourself caught in a routine? Most dad and mom do at one time or a few other but, on the time, we experience as in spite of the fact that we clearly can't get out of it. Many folks fall into a habitual as it's much much less complex and it's the same principle with cognizance and hobby. You may additionally moreover discover it a whole lot less difficult to juggle several duties or deal with distractions than you do to hobby on one specific mission till it's completed.

In fact, we've got were given had it drummed into us that multitasking is the top notch manner to get matters performed. How right is that? Well, cutting-edge studies have proven that multitasking does have a drastic impact on our art work – the incorrect impact. Not only does it make your artwork 50% worse than it should be, it furthermore will growth the time it takes to complete it via 50%. Plus, take into account it or now not, it's far honestly no longer possible, physiologically talking, for the mind to multitask.

Instead of multitasking, what you are surely doing is constantly moving your interest which kills your recognition. In fact, your thoughts actions thru three notable stages even as you multitask:

•Phase 1 – blood rush. When you begin on a challenge, the blood rushed into your anterior prefrontal cortex. In that part of your thoughts is a switchboard, a neurological one and that tells the mind that it's far approximately to shift its focus

•Phase 2 – locate/execute. That alert is an electrical rate this is made of separate parts – a seek query that is seeking out the right neurons for your mind to address the venture, and a command, which tells that neuron what it desires to do.

•Phase three – disengagement. Let's say you're writing a letter and your electronic mail alert is going. Your mind will right away disengage from the venture it's miles on and returned you go to phase 1 – the blood rush – and you start all all yet again.

This method always works in that order and in series, in no way simultaneously. That is in reality now not viable. Believe it or no longer, your thoughts can go through those degrees in on-10th of a 2d. That tells us that, first, we want to focus exquisite on one element at a time and, 2d, you want to grasp some thing known as selective interest.

Selective Attention

What makes a person smart? Surprisingly, intelligence isn't always a diploma of what's saved on your reminiscence. Instead, it is a degree of ways nicely you manipulate selective hobby. It is the ability to have entire control over the three tiers stated above.

Improving your ability to allocate your hobby selectively results for your thoughts enhancing. Your mind will discover ways to rewire itself to artwork along with your new behavior. When you pay interest difficult, you get higher at it but many people believe that, the older we get, the masses much less possibly we are if you need to selectively allocate our interest. That is truely not genuine. By doing thoughts sporting activities on a each day basis, you may sharpen your thoughts and enhance your attention and popularity competencies, irrespective of what age you are. Let's check 8 strategies to help you building up quick-time period recognition, or interest:

To start concentrating you should forestall getting distracted

That in reality is self-explanatory, don't you watched? But, but that, it genuinely is most exquisite what number of precise excuses you listen from humans as to why they will't pay hobby. Back within the 1980's, researchers requested themselves, "what came first – distraction or boredom?" Now you can be forgiven for wondering that you get distracted even as you're bored. But, in actual fact, it's far the alternative manner round. Those which may be susceptible to allowing themselves to be distracted are more likely to get bored and this means, if you need an excellent way to attention and pay attention, you have to reduce out the ones distractions.

Just one crucial interest each day

It's moreover been positioned thru scientific have a study that we sincerely can most effective awareness on one thing at a time. But, how quite a few us in reality do this? How masses people are juggling severa special jobs, have all their duties on their to-so list down as important, have to be accomplished nowadays? When you are in that scenario, when you have piles of paper to your desk, do some thing it takes to remove them. Put them in a drawer, out of sight. Then, placed your feet up, close to your eyes, and daydream.

I can see jaws losing everywhere but I'm deadly vital. Shut your eyes and ask yourself one question – what is the single maximum essential task that I should get finished in recent times. Once you have were given had been given decided that manner, do it. Do it right away on the equal time because it's sparkling to your mind. And do that every day.

Believe it or not, you may find out it lots lots less hard to consciousness and pay attention if you set your self a reason of truely one critical challenge every day, in preference to speeding round like a headless chicken, looking for to do the whole thing and in fact achieving now not a few issue besides for a mountain of strain and a thumping headache.

Think of this quote whenever you find yourself suffering to break far from multitasking! – "Don't mistake interest for success" – John Wooden

Break duties into chunks of 3

Nine instances out of ten, your one crucial task goes to need multiple motion on it. More than in all likelihood it will want several so the extraordinary problem to do is write down the entirety that you want to do to benefit it, in a logical order after which organisation them in 3 chunks.

Having a plan is the most effective manner you will effectively entire your crucial assignment and, with out one, your paintings be simply as useless as when you have been strolling round searching for to do the whole thing and attractive in no longer something.

Use a planner or to-do listing to outline your 3 separate steps, with all their separate elements, and you will obtain your purpose.

Ask inquiries to save you your self from procrastinating

When you're asked to do some thing critical, your thoughts will approach the because of this earlier than it strategies the element of the system. This is why we procrastinate — getting on with an important hobby with out statistics what you are doing or why you're doing it will probable be irritating and fruitless task.

When you discover your self procrastinating approximately some aspect, ask those questions:

Question 1 - Does this task actually must be completed?

No depend what your environment, be it in university, at art work, even at home, if you may't think about a first-rate reason why a project desires to be accomplished, ask yourself that very question. If your boss has asked you to do a job, ask them to provide an reason behind it to you, why it's so essential that it's completed right now. In that state of affairs, one in each of 4 matters will probably seem:

• Your boss will apprehend that it's just work that's keeping you busy for no purpose and you won't need to do it

• He or she can try to convince you that it need to be finished right now. If s, set yourself a quick cut-off date and get the machine accomplished

• They will provide you with a fantastically compelling cause why it is important the assignment is completed and, because of the reality you apprehend the which means that and the price of the procedure, you may be capable to complete it without troubles

• He or she might be able to lose their temper with you for asking the query. This may also want to suggest that you are operating in an area in which purpose and innovation have no location and, in case you are satisfied to art work for that kind of business enterprise, keep on. If not, discover the nearest exit!

•

Question 2 – Can I bypass this immediately to someone else to do?

If the assignment you're given has a actual due to this and a actual cause and also you in fact don't need to do it or certainly don't have the time, find out someone else who can. Trying to do a project you hate or rushing it to fit it in with the rest of your agenda is a lose-lose situation, for you and to your boss, because of the fact your paintings isn't always possibly to be up to standard.

Use some time smartly

Have you ever heard of the Pareto Principle? Sometimes known as the 80/20 principle, it works on the idea that 80% of your effectiveness is driven through the use of the use of sincerely 20% of your movements. It want to additionally be higher than that, specially whilst you are taking a seat again and remember what number of mundane responsibilities you do in a day. However, what I don't want you to do is look for the ones 20% of extensive movements and consciousness on them – it received't paintings and your mind will honestly get in a clutter and you will however become taking over way too much. Instead, as we cited earlier, stay collectively together with your one important undertaking in step with day and feature a examine to mention no to the whole lot – or in reality all and sundry-else.

There are three considered considered one of a kind varieties of people in every organization – which one are you?

•The busy individual

This is the best you word going for walks round with paper of their palms all day, working via their breaks and their vacations and continuously checking their e-mail. These are the people who are harassed past belief, those who look as despite the fact that they're workaholics however who, in real phrases, without a doubt get little or no accomplished. These are the folks who will lash out for no reason, who most usually end up with corporate burn-out.

Why does this display up? Simple — because of the truth they look busy all of the time, managers, or distinct human beings, expect that they may be the most succesful, the toughest employees. Because of that, they get more paintings assigned to them. The busy man or woman absolutely doesn't have time to do an effective undertaking and simply so they come to be turning in sub-well-known paintings. Busy human beings and workaholics are not perfect for a enterprise due to the fact they may be the least powerful worker on the payroll.

•The lazy individual

The lazy individual will blame their out of doors surroundings on their lack of capability to do their art work. In their desires they truly recognize that in the future they may be triumphant however, within the period in-between, they do not some aspect bit watch TV, devour junk food, and play video video games, all activities that release dopamine into the body. At art work, they'll deliver their time routing through the net for mundane portions of records, reaching exactly now not anything. This isn't always the kingdom you want to be in.

•The sage

The sage could be very selective about the jobs they do. They continuously ask themselves questions that most oldsters don't have time to ask. They look for giant assumptions and query every interest they may be assigned. If they turn down work, it's via a logical technique, now not because of the fact their feelings have been given within the manner.

To come to be a sage, you want to be really critical – which means that that that, everywhere you pass, you may generate the money, whether or not it's in your agency or for you. The sage is the individual that receives numerous approach gives, even supposing they're not actively attempting to find a manner.

1. Build thoughts maps

Whenever you discover yourself getting a piece overwhelmed and don't realize in which to begin, it's miles crucial that you allow you thoughts to untangle itself. You do that via building thoughts maps on paper. There are sorts – PS and Fear:

•PS Map

PS stands for trouble answer and could be a beneficial map to construct whilst you understand you need to get something finished however your thoughts has a tendency to transport in the path of a problem which you assume you have got. PS maps are essential if you are stressed and your mind maintains on racing. This is on the equal time as you begin to pace, continuously mulling a hassle over on your head. When you get to this united states of america, get a piece of paper and write a heading at the top - "problem".

Now write down all of the information of the hassle, together with the individual of it. Halfway down the paper, write every unique heading – "solution". Now write down all of the solutions you may recollect to the hassle. This is a totally smooth exercise however it permits your mind to slow down and lets you positioned perceived problems into attitude – the answer to that trouble turns into as clear as some component.

•Fear Map

Every every now and then, horrible mind get into our minds and people thoughts will very effortlessly generate fear. The manner to this is to put in writing down what the effects of that worry are and, with the aid of writing it down it'll brief come to be easy virtually how insignificant that fear without a doubt is. And, no matter the fact that the concern does even though seem considerable to you, you will recognize what the worst you can face is. Sometimes, what you trust you studied is truly the worst final results honestly isn't that awful at all.

Fear maps are quite clean and they strain you into using a logical approach for your worry. Get your piece of paper and write down the subsequent additives on it:

"If x, then y". X is your fear and y is the outcome, your estimate of what the end result of that worry may be. Through doing this, your thoughts will start to gradual down and can help you cognizance on the real mission reachable.

Find a few component in fee

Sometimes, whilst you it down to pay attention, you may effects blame your lack of potential to acquire this on an inanimate item. Remember, we noted this above, with lazy people. This isn't always a notable answer, it clearly isn't an prolonged-term one and you could't preserve on blaming some thing else in your failings. However, now and again it's difficult to get excited sufficient approximately a mission to get that blood pumping to the prefrontal cortex and, in the ones instances, an item can actually assist you.

Chapter 7: What Causes Distraction and How to Break Away

When you ultimately manage to immerse your self for your artwork, it's referred to as interest or attention. This is the element in which you are able to shut out the rest of the arena and attention all your attention at the venture in the front of you. It's what you've been aiming for, the element to your jogging day on the identical time as subjects get accomplished.

Let's face it; we are able to in no way be like this all the time. We all get distracted once in a while no matter how an entire lot we strive to combat it and it's those distractions that save you the mind from focusing on what wishes to be finished, whether or not it's at home or artwork. But, do you apprehend what's in truth moving into inner your thoughts at the same time as you are concentrating? Do you know how to educate your mind to get into that usa of interest?

This monetary destroy is all about understanding interest and attention and, likely extra importantly, distractions. To apprehend why you get distracted, you need to understand how your mind works and, after you recognize that, you can art work on reducing those distractions out and training your mind to pay interest better. At the prevent of the day, hobby is a skill and its one which takes time and exercising to increase.

What takes place on your mind whilst you're each focused and distracted?

We mentioned this in brief before but now I need to go into greater element approximately what occurs on your thoughts and I'm going to begin with at the same time as you are concentrating or that specialize in a few issue and then what takes place whilst that recognition is damaged. As you could see, each of the strategies are clearly intertwined.

What takes place on the identical time as you recognition:

When you attention on a mission, your brain goes through two fundamental steps. This is quite a whole lot the identical whether or not the point of interest is voluntary or involuntary. Selective cognizance comes beneath the control of the pinnacle-down attention tool. This is without a doubt underneath your manage and incorporates one smooth query – "what's it you want to awareness on?" When you're making the selection that you're going to popularity on a particular element, the mind needs to type after which apprehend the records and it does it in those steps:

• In a seen way, i.E. Via the eyes, you notice the data within the front of you and you begin to way it. You do this to try and decide what you need to pay the most interest to. Imagine it as a photograph or a photo this is blurred and that starts offevolved to easy and are to be had into reputation.

• The 2d a part of the approach entails your recognition on one component – the bit you want to be privy to. Think once more to that burry phot – because it comes into attention, your interest will choose out one a part of the image in case you want to recognition on

When you're for your focused zone, your complete perception of what's taking area around you changes and you find out that your functionality to dam out and neglect approximately things is lots sharper. This is referred to as being "in the place" and it's while you are so centered that not anything round you enters your worldwide until soothing suggestions the stability and kicks off your bottom-up interest gadget. We'll talk extra approximately that in a second however first, permit's check what honestly befell to your mind from a mental point of view.

When you're focused, each additives of your thoughts are going for walks together, pretty thankfully and pretty effectively and are able to block out what's taking place round you. Your experience of time disappears and you appear to come to be at one with the venture you're targeting. This is much like a trance-like us of a.

What takes vicinity whilst you harm attention?

The idea of breaking your awareness is one this is primarily based mostly on an a long time-vintage device this is designed to maintain you safe. Selective recognition is based at the pinnacle-down attention machine wherein breaking your interest relies on the bottom-up device. Where you control pinnacle-down, you can not manage bottom-up because of the fact it's miles difficult-stressed out for your thoughts and is a totally passive manner. Bottom-up hobby asks the query – "what goes on that requires my hobby?"

There are important events an extraordinary manner to cause you to interrupt your interest – loud sounds and colorful shades or bright lights. Your interest is robotically drawn in the course of whatever that might be profitable or unstable – take into account an animal growling, a police siren or the sounds of a carnival passing your window.

As quickly as your pinnacle-down interest has been broken it could take you upwards of 25 mins to regain it. Every time it gets damaged, you have to begin all all all over again and, in the technique, your mind's property are used up. Effectively, you've got were given end up exhausted. Picture a glass of water – this is your interest tool.

When it is undisturbed you may see at once thru it and you could supply hobby to at least one undertaking. Hit or knock it and it will become disturbed and then it takes a while to loosen up once more enough so you can see via it all over again. As time goes by way of, that water evaporated and by the time the stop of the day comes, there's no longer something left. This brings us to the subsequent trouble – a way to determine what those distractions are and dispose of the triggers so you can factor your recognition where it wants to be.

What breaks your interest and the way do you get spherical it?

We are all one-of-a-kind and it's highly in all likelihood that, in a few unspecified time in the future at some point of your lifestyles, you have were given got met a person who is able to give attention to analyzing a e-book at the same time as the TV is on or who can supply attention to their art work with the tune going entire pelt. When it comes for your very very own awareness, you need to pinpoint those triggers that motive it to break and discover ways to do away with them for extended blocks of time. Let's take a more in-depth study the two distraction reasons we cited earlier.

How to reduce outside distractions

We apprehend that there are sincerely two kinds of distraction for you to motive you to break your popularity – mild and sound. Being able to minimize the ones distractions is a first rate manner of ensuring that now not some thing can get for your interest and break it. There are plenty of methods to block out outside belongings of distraction and, in case you go searching the internet, you'll find out masses of diverse corporations and apps which might be constructed on this idea. Here I surely have a few simple guidelines that will let you to block out a good buy of the outside distractions: Wear a couple of headphones or a few earplugs

If your biggest purpose for distraction is loud noises, pop a couple of headphones on ar some earplugs. That will do away with them out of your location of popularity; try the noise cancelling variations as they paintings the first rate. Do undergo in thoughts that those loud noises are not continuously directed at you. Sometimes, the noise may be sincerely outside and no longer regarding you in any respect. Any noise this is loud is sufficient to interrupt your consciousness but, if you can't precisely pinpoint what the trouble is, take a recorder in and report your entire day. Play it decrease again at the same time as you get home and also you ought to be able to pay attention what the distractions are and if they arrive at particular times of the day. If they are subjects which may be scheduled which encompass the furnace drawing close, you could artwork some time desk round them. If it's miles in reality standard noise, get the headphones on for while you need to cognizance without any distractions.

Use digital blinders

Of direction you could't located real blinders on at the equal time as you're focusing due to the fact you wouldn't be able to see but you could do away with visible cues which can be round you that you could discover distracting. This approach you need to block out each seen and audio notifications. Notifications are distracting, there may be no procedures approximately it. Turn your mobile phone onto silent and urn off vibrate; many smartphones can help you set timers on notifications nowadays so if yours does, use them. Turn off your e mail so you don't maintain getting pinged at the same time as one is available in. In fact flip off a few element that sends you notifications and turn off the ringer on your table cellular phone – you may continuously divert it to someone else for a while and they could come get you if it's urgent. Do be smooth in your which means of urgent even though!

How to restrict inner distractions

Most, if no longer every body, are distracted in some unspecified time in the future at some level in the day with the beneficial resource of internal thoughts. Perhaps it is probably which you marvel what to have for dinner; you marvel why you said what you probable did on your boss this morning or why the female within the coffee store became in a lousy temper. Whatever it's miles, you could do subjects to limit the ones mind wanderings on every occasion you need your interest on a selected undertaking.

It's clean enough to set your surroundings up so that you don't get disturbed by way of manner of outside distractions however it's going to take real commitment to shut out your internal belief techniques. It isn't smooth however it's far feasible.

First you need to be simply aware about your idea strategies and try to capture keep of the impulse to don't forget some thing else, earlier than you surely do. Timing in truth is everything in this example – as soon as you have got got started out out to perform a little factor, it genuinely may be very hard to break that loop. Let's say you consider you studied to your self, I'm without a doubt going to look if that essential commercial enterprise enterprise electronic mail has are to be had in. You open your email and it hasn't but, hey, you have three new messages from pals. Once you see them it's very hard to take the choice that you are not going to have a look at them but that's precisely what you have to do. Perhaps you make a decision that you're going to upward push up and skip – the minute that preference is made, subjects begin to appear – regions of your mind begin taking walks, blood starts offevolved offevolved pumping in anticipation of you transferring and, get hold of as actual with me, it's an lousy lot tougher to save you yourself from getting up than it's miles to go together with the drift. In order to forestall your self from turning into distracted, you want to learn how to stop those behavior from forming within the first place.

While it's a brilliant aspect to learn how to cope with all of the distractions you face, an first rate higher issue, specially inside the long term, is to educate your brain the manner to hobby extra efficiently.

Use the Power of Science to Focus

It takes a bargain of schooling to learn how to attention properly. If you convert your surroundings to in shape and train your mind, you will discover that it turns into increasingly more less difficult to cognizance even as you want to. As well due to the fact the above examples I gave you to developing an first-rate surroundings, I sincerely have some greater thoughts to assist educate your mind to slide into recognition mode without any real try to your behalf:

Make the assignment you have got were given to finish more relevant

This is simply a totally easy concept. We recognize that when we are focused we are using the top-down interest device and this is the crucial factor device in any to-do list. Simply placed the maximum vital component at the top of the list and the least crucial all of the manner down the bottom. Take the undertaking you apprehend you need to reputation on these days – positioned it proper away to the top of the listing and supply it a brief reduce-off date. At the same time, provide yourself a praise for finishing it through the reduce-off date. With a to-do list, you region all your recognition on the venture on the pinnacle of the listing and to make yourself consciousness better, place more significance on that unique mission.

Use meditation

Scientific research have indicated that meditation is right for constructing up the mind tissue across the additives of the thoughts which can be associated with interest. The studies had been searching at the extended-term results however they do show that the mind is trainable and that meditation may be used to teach the thoughts a way to attention higher,

Before you get hung up on having to analyze all the ones hard things you have got look at about meditation, there are much less hard strategies to do it. The first step is to learn how to deliver hobby in your respiratory and blocking your mind out. This is one of the key factors in studying the way to prevent your mind from wandering, the way to keep your self centered. These are the very first steps in meditation, the primary topics you may examine in any elegance or from any internet website online. Even if you can't see your manner clean to going all the way with meditation, make certain you at least observe that.

Easy mind training – have a look at a superb e-book

When you attention your mind on something that is efficient, it triggers off the same areas of the thoughts which you use to interest on a few element that is lovely. So, turn this round. In order to discover ways to popularity on vital obligations, use entertainment as a shape of education. One of the remarkable techniques to do this is to lose your self in an excellent e-book, to the amount that you are ignorant of the phrase round you – this is genuine attention.

At the quit of the day, there definitely isn't any differentiation in the varieties of assets you reputation on. Whether it's miles art work, a extraordinary film or e book, or that photograph you've been making plans to paint, the give up aim is the identical – recognition. In any interest you adopt, there can be the capability to transport from being simply engaged, to bored and having a wandering mind. We all apprehend at the same time as we're specializing in a few element completely because it takes no attempt to do it.

It doesn't virtually remember number what form of amusement you use. Not every body reads however the factor is, something you do it need to be difficult and you need to be doing it actively. TV isn't so unique because of the everyday ad breaks however in case you watch a film, play a pastime or look at a e-book, they'll be right techniques of bringing escapism into your lifestyles as a way of schooling your thoughts the manner to consciousness. The key factor is, you need to be actively centered on a few element you are doing. That method no placing the ebook down to test your Facebook web page, no pausing the movie to take a look at your emails. Shut out the lights and all distractions and enjoy your form of leisure thoroughly.

Let me really get one element easy. Running thru the ones bodily sports activities isn't always going to make it feasible to be able to right now run off and pay hobby actually on a large mission. Instead they're designed to get you into the sensation of attention and consciousness, of a manner to disregard distractions and the way to replace that to all which you do, whilst you need to.

Understanding how your mind focuses is the important component to reading the way to teach it to awareness and set apart the ones distractions. Once you've learnt it, never allow it escape from you yet again.

Chapter 8: The Focus Myth

Focus. Many people pay attention this word nowadays and recollect priests in a ways flung monasteries or extraordinarily-marathoners that run for days on stop. Maybe everybody need extra interest in our lives, but that's for special humans without jobs, families, and rush-hour traffic. We snort and add it to the bottom of the listing, beneath spending the night time in a bubble bath or curling up with a ebook.

Being able to attention feels more elusive than prevailing the lottery. Believe it or now not, this is what the sector wants you to accept as true with. The longer we spend distracted with the aid of our favourite television indicates, the more commercials we see and the extra agencies advantage. This digital worldwide is designed to tell us that focus is unbelievable and that we haven't any one-of-a-kind choice however to cut up our time among productiveness and distraction.

Despite knowledge what desires to be finished thru the surrender of each day, we revel in pulled in every direction. Even even as we sooner or later art work up the inducement to sit down down and start our taxes, we prompt the computer and word an alert about a chum's birthday. One click on on a buying net website to shop for a present outcomes in an insatiable urge to buy a current day cleaning soap dish. Hours skip, the closing date techniques, and the attraction of social media receives more potent. We make friends with a large pot of espresso and spend the middle of the night in a tug-of-battle most of the given venture and the whole lot else the world has to offer. Who knew there were such a number of motion snap shots of cats falling into bathtubs?

But what if I tell you that it's miles all a myth? Focus is there in every 2d, without a doubt ready a good way to use it. No depend the motion of distractions flowing thru your day, you have entire manipulate over it sluggish and the manner you spend it. Focus remains attention and it hasn't changed for the motive that first day that the caveman sat right right right down to construct a hearth. The exquisite difference in recent times is that we need to be savvy approximately trapping reputation and no longer letting it stray.

This ebook is for folks that need to benefit manipulate of their productiveness through coming across the factors that make up their specific attention formulation. Using smooth strategies designed to maximize time and hobby, it becomes easy that modest changes can produce massive effects. We will examine the entirety from the construction of your to-do listing to the strategic integration of sports you experience into a while desk. We will learn how to well hyperlink your lengthy-term desires in your quick-term desires so that you can increase motivation and a manner to properly shape your view of the triumphing 2d to get you thru your most daunting and dreadful duties. With this e-book, you can learn how to shape your consciousness additives definitely so it's far effortlessly carried out into your every day lifestyles and maximum tough obligations. This is your adventure and the place spherical you is your manual.

How to Use This Book

This book is designed to equip you with the system critical to craft a life-style in which you experience on pinnacle of things of your very personal awareness and productiveness. Through the improvement of a focal point device, you will study what that way of life looks like for you. Whether you're a commercial enterprise proprietor with many years of records seeking to revamp your techniques, or you're a pupil looking to stay on your final assessments, the ones strategies will help you discern the way to optimize the focal point for your life through being attentive to your herbal pastimes, dislikes, and productivity dispositions.

Focus is particular to all of us, and so too might be your journey thru this e-book. Some may additionally locate it useful to take a look at from the primary net page to the ultimate, and others may additionally want to jump spherical. Some might also furthermore want to finish the bodily video games on their computer systems, on the same time as others might also additionally need to apply a mag to allow for in addition reflection. Regardless of your opportunities, I might propose transcribing the bodily sports right into a separate laptop record or pocket ebook so you can add to them as wished. The extra thorough you're with the bodily video games, the more notion you may gain concerning your awareness desires. This ebook is designed for you and, as such, desires to fulfill your desires. Feel free to conform and manipulate these techniques and physical video games as you note in form. This is your hobby machine and the effectiveness of it will likely be contemplated via the perception and paintings you positioned into growing it.

Even on this distracting international, there may be no excuse for being unfocused and unproductive. You are in the driving force's seat of your non-public life and, with the ones strategies, you will become higher prepared to steer in the path of your selecting. Remember which you are on pinnacle of factors. There's now not some element stopping you from making these days the maximum centered and efficient day you have got were given ever had. Focus isn't always a miracle, however the outcomes aren't some thing brief of first-rate. So, examine on and allow's get commenced.

Chapter 9: Defining Focus

Open the dictionary and you'll discover a definition of consciousness. Write it on a massive piece of paper, tape it to the wall inside the the the front of your desk, and phone it a day, right? Not so speedy. Assuming that one definition will serve a big range of desires is like assuming that one avenue will bring about Los Angeles, New York City, and Philadelphia. While reputation may be a hard and fast up purpose, the way it manifests itself in daily life appears tremendous from man or woman to man or woman and scenario to state of affairs.

Imagine that a songwriter and a college professor had to proportion an place of job cubicle for an afternoon. After debates of who receives to sit toward the air con, each pull out their materials and get to art work. It isn't lengthy in advance than the songwriter is distracted via the piles of papers which might be crowding his region, and the professor is protective his palms in his ears so as not to hear the identical lyrics repeated time and again once more at each feasible tempo and tone. The day ends and the most effective issue that each has completed is getting a headache.

The hassle isn't that songwriters and professors have an innate hatred for every considered one of a type. Despite their variations, I'm sure the 2 might also find out every wonderful charming at a dinner party. Instead, it's probable that the 2 have very wonderful definitions of popularity. While cognizance to a songwriter could likely entail being attentive to a chunk of exertions on repeat, a professor could possibly want natural silence. While the songwriter may additionally simplest need his laptop and guitar, the professor famous it beneficial to make notes on portions of scrap paper with a huge pink pen. Similar to the way everybody have outstanding alternatives, desires, and goals, we all have special desires almost about enlisting the intellectual wherewithal to complete a undertaking.

It might also moreover moreover seem obvious that a songwriter and a professor also can additionally run into conflicts whilst going for walks in the equal region. However, this hassle is simply as ordinary among people with the same aim or even with the equal undertaking. Do you keep in mind your university days at the same time as you idea that studying collectively with your brilliant buddy in your tests was an notable concept? Although you may also were unstoppable at the basketball court docket or at a celebration, I bet your grades suffered.

In order to begin the approach of building your focus system, we want to begin at rectangular one and determine what attention manner. This definition may be unique to you and will probable trade relying on the assignment and environment. Maybe traditional rock locations you within the proper mood to complete that final bicep curl on the gymnasium, whilst u . S . Is what receives you thru a tough run on the trail. Don't get connected to 1 idea of popularity; be organized for it to alternate as your desires and desires alternate.

There's no doubt that you have already got some idea of at the same time as and why you're targeted in sure situations. This ebook does not run on the presumption that you are a easy slate with out a enjoy of your personal interest functionality. The purpose is to take your modern information, increase it, and make it paintings even higher for you. To get us started out out, I need you to write down down down your definition of reputation as it relates to a variety of duties. This can each be what it manner to you or what contributes to it. Although handiest slots are supplied, revel in loose to feature as many obligations and definitions as wished. We will revisit the ones definitions on the surrender of the e-book to look how they've modified.

Why We Need Focus

This also can appear obvious. Without interest, we might all want to-do lists longer than our driveways and in no way get round to converting our socks. Despite all of the distractions the sector has to offer through social media, generation, and the first rate outside, we all have enough attention to get thru our each day lives without falling into open manholes. In short, we have were given enough focus to do what's anticipated and get to the subsequent birthday with some accomplishments within the bucket. Herein lies the trouble. Our popularity is simply appropriate sufficient to blind us from what we can be sporting out if it changed into at its tremendous. Maybe we stayed up all night time in a crazed daze finishing that report, but the fact that we sooner or later finished it's miles all that we care approximately. Rarely do we prevent and remember what else we have to have done that night time time if we hadn't needed to conflict such a variety of distractions and had spent more time targeted at the mission on hand.

Focus is what separates the good from the first-rate. It's easy that staying up all night time to finish a report is proper, however completing the document and spending the relaxation of the night with the circle of relatives or getting a jumpstart on tomorrow's work is high-quality. We pay attention testimonies every day about marketers which have commenced groups in their garages in a rely of weeks. What seems like years of hard paintings may be expedited while the time spent on target films, e-mails, and on line shopping for is positioned to higher use. To positioned it more in reality, your capacity to recognition proper away translates into your capability to carry out your goals. Every minute you spend on some issue extraneous is a minute you're no longer spending strolling on a few element good sized to you.

The Numbers

When the state of affairs of consciousness comes up at dinner events, a person continually brings up the problem of time. If great we had sufficient hours in the day to complete everything that desires to be completed. If best the tv would possibly prevent turning on magically. If great someone ought to create a system to freeze time. It is right that it might be a lucky stroke of magic for a person to invent a manner to provide us all limitless amounts of time. I don't do not forget, no matter the reality that, that this would assist our potential to cognizance. In fact, as we can speak later, having extra time can also surely be a focal point killer. Regardless, we are all beneath the affect that we've too little time in our days and that is why we are falling short on our to-do lists. If we certainly do take into account this so passionately, permit's indulge in the concept and take a look at the numbers. Let's see if we have been accurate all along and a lack of time in reality is in rate for our lack of ability to cognizance.

There are 7 days in every week, which suits out to 168 hours. Let's say that you paintings a ordinary 40 hours each week. This leaves you with 128 hours to do with as you please. Assuming you haven't decided the magical spell that makes dozing vain, allow's be beneficiant and wish which you are napping as a minimum 7 hours a night time time. Forty-9 hours of sleep factored into your week leaves you with seventy nine hours to journey, prepare dinner dinner dinner, pick out out your kids up from college, smooth the house, or perform a little detail amusing for a trade. Seventy-9 hours. If the rumor is proper that walking a circle of relatives and having a own family is type of an entire-time manner and a 1/2, allow's take out 60 hours to account for that duty. You despite the fact that have 19 hours left for your week unaccounted for. Now, I comprehend that sudden time wasters pop up each day. The vehicle breaks down, the kids come down with the flu, or your boss asks you to complete a challenge after hours. Life happens and it often doesn't suit into the time desk. However, regardless of how the universe conspires within the course of you, 19 hours every week is lots of time.

A 2012 article in The Atlantic1 discovered that the greater hours people art work every week, the much more likely they'll be to exaggerate the sort of hours they spent running. This isn't to mention that we are deliberately mendacity, but that our perceptions of approaches we spend our time are frequently faulty. This can be specifically proper if we are doing subjects we don't experience. Haven't you ever felt that the twenty mins you spent in the dentist's chair felt longer than the two hours you spent searching your favourite film? Without monitoring, our beliefs approximately how we spend our time can be advocated through our emotions related to the assignment. If we step lower back and recognise that our frame of human beings meeting felt like five hours, however changed into amazing two hours in truth, we are capable of forestall blaming our lack of time on our jobs and understand that we wasted greater than an hour getting to know kale recipes. No rely your venture, if a -hour employees meeting often looks like five hours, and also you spend extra time at your table making playlists in your subsequent road adventure than completing obligations, it is able to be time for a lifestyles alternate.

By misinterpreting how a super deal time we spend on responsibilities, we run the threat of upfront fatiguing our popularity. Your mind is educated to apply time as a hallmark of the attempt it's going to need to exert to complete a assignment. The belief approach behind strolling for twenty minutes is a lot tremendous than the concept manner in the back of walking for two hours. By priming it to assume greater than is needed, you are likely to empty your recognition really by way of thinking about the assignment on hand. I should spend extra time fretting over walking for two hours than for twenty minutes and might in all likelihood revel in exhausted earlier than even setting my footwear on. You'll be surprised to peer that the clean trick of as it ought to be calculating how a wonderful deal time you spend finishing obligations can enhance cognizance with the useful aid of proscribing intellectual fatigue this is introduced on via faux perceptions.

Use the chart under (or a sheet of pocket book paper) to report the quantity of time you spend interacting with numerous additives of your life. Be as outstanding as possible and file the quantity of time you spend finishing particular obligations. For instance, in desire to writing that you paintings from 9 to five, write what you usually do all through that factor. Maybe you usually have a meeting from ten to eleven, a lunch break from eleven to twelve, a convention call from twelve to at least one, and so on and so on. The greater actual you're, the less complex it's far going to be to replace the perceptions of the manner you spend some time with the fact. This will provide you with a basis to work from as we flow into earlier with the point of interest strategies.

Monday:

_____

_____

Tuesday:

_____

_____

Wednesday:

_____

_____

Thursday:

_____

_____

Friday:

_____

_____

Saturday:

_____

_____

Sunday:

_____

_____

Chapter 10: Remembering the "Why"

"Because I stated so," is a word this is used all too frequently whilst explaining the need of a undertaking. Even if you haven't heard that phrase due to the fact you've got been five, bear in mind all of the times it is implied in each day sports activities. We put together files in a certain style because of the reality that is the way it has typically been completed, we recite sure prayers at church due to the fact anyone has finished so for years, and we make Grandma's coffeecake with that one cake pan as it wouldn't be the equal otherwise. While this could seem unrelated to recognition and talk absolutely to our evolution as creatures of addiction, failing to recognize the reasons within the returned of our movements has horrible implications for our productivity.

Habits are commonly dull. While we may be thankful that we've professional ourselves to brush our teeth every day, it's not something to get too captivated with. The recognition we showcase within the ones moments is not the same popularity on the way to get us through writing an prolonged fee report. While one demonstrates our robotic-like inclinations, the alternative requires more concept. We need to need to install writing that fee file as badly as we want to leap into the satisfactory and relaxed blue ocean verified on that adventure display approximately Hawaii. We want a purpose why.

Desire is the excellent friend of recognition. The extra we want some thing, the extra hard we are willing to paintings for it. Recall the traditional movie scene of the man or woman strolling thru the airport, dodging safety guards, and scaling terminal walls as a manner to reach the female he loves earlier than her flight leaves. If you requested him why he have turn out to be developing a fool of himself within the airport, I doubt he might in all likelihood hesitate for even a 2nd in advance than telling you. "Why" is the maximum powerful and maximum effective tool in our attention toolkits. We want to understand the motivations at the back of our actions and the way they relate to our dreams. There's no questioning why the Hawaiian ocean is so appealing and, in order to finish that charge report, your conviction wants to be simply as strong.

Clarifying

It is straightforward to lose focus on a mission while the "why" of it is uncertain. Although counterintuitive, this most often takes place even as we are going for walks on obligations related to our biggest and most prized dreams. While we can also moreover need now not a few aspect greater than to run a marathon, on that first day of training, while even miles is more than we will control, the "why" is all that keeps us tying up our shoes every day. The clarity of our "why" right away translates into the amount of awareness we located right right right into a task.

I'm going to light up this detail with the aid of introducing you to Neil, a chum which will examine us during the the rest of the e-book. Neil is an assistant to a very good CEO at the economic company employer of his goals. As a lower-degree employee, Neil often well-known himself tasked with assignments that aren't inherently large to him, however are crucial if he wants to pass up the professional ladder, reach his interest, and gain his large desires. One of these dreams is turning into a CEO of a large organisation himself sooner or later. This goal, notwithstanding the truth that far off, may be used to increase Neil's popularity on duties he wants to end nowadays if he can make clear the "why" in the lower lower back of looking to emerge as a CEO within the first region.

Goals which may be a number of years down the road can come to be precis and fairy-tale like. Becoming a CEO is to date from Neil's contemporary fact, he doesn't understand what this sort of life could consist of. He imagines a flowery car, an expensive match, and a luxurious coffeemaker searching out him each morning as he wakes up in his European silk sheets. He sees himself taking element in business enterprise journeys to extremely good places, constructing a strong team spherical him, and passing on his information to the subsequent generation of leaders. It is feasible that this is what Neil's life will appear like. With his desires and pressure, there's no doubt that he'll locate himself in the nook place of job at some point.

The hassle is that such prolonged-time period visions of future desires can emerge as hackneyed if left within the summary global of delusion and may be of no company whilst the going gets tough. Let's say that Neil has a horrific day at work and is questioning his desire to hold down the course of CEO. In this moment, envisioning himself in a awesome in form and the usage of an expensive automobile will become extra of a cool animated film and a mockery than a motivation. This vision of himself seems thus far from his contemporary reality that it demoralizes him similarly in desire to reinvigorating him. Instead of that specialize in his paintings for the day, he reveals that his assignments seem unimportant and the contemporary basketball ratings pull his attention. Basketball is right here and now, at the equal time as CEO is dream.

Neil has flawed the aspect consequences of undertaking his aim for the "why" of pursuing it. Although he may also moreover moreover revel in exquisite airline tickets as soon as he is bumped to CEO recognition, this is sincerely a element impact of his success. It's similar to receiving a free air freshener at the same time as you buy a contemporary car. The air freshener is a nice perk however not why you got the car inside the first place. Similarly, Neil's pricey lifestyle may be a pleasant issue impact of his promotion to CEO, however no longer the reason why he's pursuing the intention in the first region.

By mistakenly focusing on element results in area of "whys," we lose music of our motivations. Our goals come to be based absolutely upon cloth desires rather than values and lose their attraction as a end result. Although the pursuit of coins can seem for ever and ever motivating, it received't get you thru the ones hard days in the identical way that values and beliefs will. If you don't consider me, reflect onconsideration on the ultimate time you splurged on a pal's birthday, went to that live performance you'd been dreaming of, or maxed out a credit score rating card to buy an airline price tag to visit family at the vacations. Commitment to dwelling an notable lifestyles constantly wins over having an entire financial institution account. When it comes all the manner right right down to it, we select values over coins and cloth possessions 99 percentage of the time. This is why dreams which might be focused on side consequences will now not be as motivating as dreams that have smooth "whys" that hook up with non-public values.

This is not to mention which you want to overlook approximately the flowery motors and super holidays. Side consequences have their region, but it's far essential to differentiate them from motivations. Doing so will will let you entertain the fantasies of a life of success, even as not difficult that myth at the side of your reasons for pursing the goal.

Use the chart below to help you differentiate among your motivations for pursing a purpose and the thing outcomes an exceptional way to end result from achieving it. For Neil, truly certainly one of his motivations for becoming CEO is to grow to be a mentor to more youthful enterprise employer executives as they start their journeys, at the same time as a facet effect might be a brand new sports activities automobile.

Goal:

_____

_____

Motivation:

_____

_____

Side Effects:

_____

_____

Although we examined clarifying your "why" because it relates to refocusing on large dreams, the equal method can be applied to smaller desires as properly. Let's say that Neil has clarity on his reason to emerge as a CEO, but he struggles to live centered on his purpose to prepare dinner dinner for himself on a regular basis. Every day it's miles the same tale. Neil returns from a long day at work, opens his empty refrigerator, and reveals the take-out menu greater attractive than slaving over the variety.

This motive seems small in assessment to the one of becoming a CEO, however the identical ideas take a look at. Neil desires to domestic in on his motivations for looking to prepare dinner dinner for himself within the first vicinity and the aspect effects of doing so. If he struggles to try this, connecting this smaller purpose to a larger intention may additionally additionally have the same refocusing outcomes. Let's say that Neil buddies cooking dinner for himself each night to his professional achievement. Perhaps the thing consequences of saving cash on food that lets in you to return from cooking every day will better permit him to spend money on his professional fabric cupboard and connect with his motivations of becoming a expert authority figure as a CEO. By linking his smaller motive to his big cause, he not high-quality clarifies his recognition but moreover creates a web of goals. The more you're able to intertwine your dreams, the a great deal much less difficult it will likely be to keep music of your motivations and preserve attention.

Redefining

There are times at the identical time as a lack of recognition isn't due to the truth that the "why" of a reason desires to be clarified, however that it desires an entire overhaul. There are many reasons for doing some thing in existence and discovering the proper reason is prime to keeping popularity and motivation on attaining your reason. For instance, you can take out the trash because of the fact the can is complete or to delight your partner. Both of these are legitimate reasons for putting off the trash, however attractive your accomplice may be greater vital to you than having an empty rubbish can. As such, redefining your "why" of getting rid of the trash to pleasing your companion in region of the need of emptying the can will make extra experience to your trendy goals of supporting your circle of relatives, if you want to gain your capabilities to interest at the venture. In his modern assistant characteristic, Neil is anticipated to write a report every month highlighting the organization's improvement and the modifications that have befell because the month earlier. This is an task that Neil dreads and struggles to complete. He doesn't view himself as a writer and exhibits it difficult to sit down down all the way all the manner down to a easy computer show at the same time as tasked with something as stupid as a monthly document. Every month he receives swept up within the ultra-contemporary-day basketball recreation, falls into the lure of answering unimportant e-mails, wastes hours on social media, and ultimately finally ends up staying up all night time time writing a record that could have only taken three hours if he can also moreover need to have stayed centered.

As Neil dreads report writing, he hasn't belief about the "why" of it past the reality that it's far in his pastime description and his boss expects it of him every month. The "why" of writing his document is as essential to him due to the fact the "why" of converting the smooth out in his vacuum, which he doesn't do with regularity. It is dull, tedious, and a waste of time. Neil desires to redefine the "why" of his report writing in order that it includes extra weight and relates to his desires.

When going thru a mission which you are struggling to popularity on, redefine it in order that it is driven via the usage of your private dreams. Neil sees the significance of document writing for his professional improvement, however connects the "why" greater so you can his boss than to himself. The record is some thing his boss calls for, units the expectations for, and in the end advantages from. When redefining the "why" of his reviews, Neil focuses on himself instead of his boss. He tells himself that the act of writing will enhance the verbal exchange talents he goes to want as he movements up the ladder. Analyzing the organisation's month-to-month development will alert him to the factors that contribute to a a achievement business employer. And the improvement of a portfolio of written critiques will feature precious proof of his competence as he asks for a vending. By redefining his file writing with a more private reputation, Neil is capable of be a part of it to his desires and finds it a lot much less complex to attention as a result. Instead of falling prey to distractions, at the same time as Neil sits all of the way all of the way down to write, he's privy to how his evaluations will immediately impact his capability to end up a CEO in the destiny. No longer is he serving nice the desires of his boss, however he is likewise serving his personal desires.

When you're struggling to stay targeted on a venture, remember whether or not or no longer or no longer you want to redefine your motives for pursuing it. Use the chart below to redefine the "whys" of dreams you've got been suffering to attention on. Be positive which you make your "whys" non-public and unique with the intention to great boom your recognition on hard duties.

Task:_____

_____

Previous
"Why":_____

_____

Redefined
"Why":_____

_____

Crafting

Unfortunately, existence isn't generally whole of full-size and interesting duties. There are instances at the equal time as, regardless of the manner you redefine your "why," a task nonetheless appears dreadful and now not well worth a while. This is how I experience whenever my chemical rest room purifier begins offevolved giving me the stink eye, and I turn my decrease decrease again to observe greater television. These are the responsibilities for which interest is so elusive that stalling to complete them takes on a life of its personal. Eventually, my green sink will start to detour pals, scare away circle of relatives pets, and leave me brushing my teeth out of doors on the reduce, however plunging through the dust seems now not possible. In moments like those, it's time to get modern.

In those moments even as your popularity is to date lengthy past that you can't even supply yourself to get started out out out on a undertaking, pick out a motive and inform yourself a tale approximately how the challenge is important on your fulfillment in that purpose. Your purpose and your challenge need no longer additionally be inherently associated. For example, if I battle to easy my rest room on a weekly basis, I can tell myself a tale of techniques completing this mission will advantage my purpose of scripting this e book. If I really have a clean relaxation room, I will spend much less time complaining about the mess, spring away from bed more short, take tons much less time getting prepared, and be at my laptop in an entire lot tons an awful lot less time.

Be affected individual as you use this approach. It seems illogical that cleaning my lavatory will effect my very last contact of this e-book, but the greater instances I tell myself it is so, the extra I will come to don't forget it. Stories are powerful and the memories we inform ourselves have the capability to form our behaviors. Neil, for example, will start to take delivery of as actual with that cooking dinner for himself is important to his fulfillment as a CEO if he tells himself that the meditative act of decreasing veggies places him inside the calm mindset essential for focusing on his opinions and one-of-a-kind administrative responsibilities. Soon, cooking dinner for himself can be inextricably related to his professional success.

This technique may sound crazy, however do not forget how deeply we acquire as proper with in miracles and fairy stories. Even our most logical selves hold onto small threads of want that the wizards we take a look at about in our favorite delusion novels honestly exist in a few some distance-off land. Your capacity to interest on a assignment relies upon upon how strongly associated you experience to the tale you inform yourself approximately it. Think approximately how focused you've got been at some point of your using test as a teen. The story you instructed yourself approximately freedom, independence, and adulthood changed into so powerful that your interest emerge as no longer something quick of high-quality as you made those left turns.

When suffering to cognizance on a project due to its loss of meaning and importance to you, inform yourself a tale about why that assignment is important on your achievement in considered certainly one of your maximum coveted dreams. As absurd because the tale may additionally moreover sound, inform yourself on a each day foundation that it's miles authentic. Before prolonged, you'll find your self believing it and your functionality to recognition to your undertaking will skyrocket. Use the chart underneath to link your obligations to a goal and to tell your self a tale approximately why they're primarily based upon each notable.

Task → Goal:

_____

_____

Story:

_____

_____

_____

_____

_____

_____

Yours vs. Theirs

There isn't always any arguing that extended-term commitments can be tons less fun than brief-term ones. This is why we are so attracted to immediately gratification. This is also why, even as supplied with a miles an awful lot much less than appropriate challenge, we are brief to dismiss it. Neil, as an instance, is aware of that the direction to CEO might be painful. It may be masses more fantastic inside the quick-time period to dismiss his file, stay in his modern role, push aside his efforts for vending, and watch sports activities activities activities all night time time. This is a trouble that would frequently be rectified with the aid of clarifying, redefining, and crafting the "whys" at the back of your dreams and duties. If, but, you have got moved thru all 3 steps and despite the fact that can't regain reputation for your responsibilities, it's possible that your desires are not your non-public.

There's a huge difference amongst desires you need for your self and people which have been imposed upon you with the resource of own family, buddies, and society. Sometimes they're one and the identical, however be searching out those who aren't. Maybe your own family of teachers raised you to bear in mind that this sort of profession end up the most effective direction to success, or society's obsession with yoga satisfied you that nice health have to best be carried out after efficaciously reading a headstand. Whether huge or small, silly or extreme, desires that are not your personal will serve as distracters at the same time as trying to interest on responsibilities. If becoming a CEO is a aim that became imposed on him through his father, Neil will not best struggle to focus on his monthly file but will in all likelihood abandon it altogether. If the project is for my part meaningless, and the motive it's far linked to is in my opinion meaningless as properly, popularity stands little risk of winning the war.

Sometimes it isn't always so clean to differentiate amongst your desires and people imposed on you by way of using others. Neil, as an instance, can also have heard his father talk about the merits of expert control from such an early age that he commenced to count on it modified into what he desired for himself. The key to differentiating amongst your in my view imposed desires and those imposed by way of others is figuring out the "why" of every. If your "why" involves you fast, it might be yours. In addition, if your "why" is associated with you, it's miles in all likelihood yours.

Now, this could sound obvious, however goals which might be imposed by using the usage of others frequently have an externally targeted "why" or a "why" that sounds not unusual. For instance, if you grew up in a circle of relatives of instructors, however you don't need to be a trainer yourself, your "why" for turning into a instructor may be, "Teachers make a distinction within the lives of children," rather than, "I need to share my love for technological knowledge and encourage the following technology of inventors." The latter is much more likely to encourage your interest on studying on your coaching credential checks than the former. If your "whys" are installation and unrelated to you, it's time to both refine your desires or ditch them for contemporary ones.

Use the chart below to find out the "whys" of your goals. Feel free to write down each quick- and long-term goals, as even brief-term desires can fall into the lure of societal expectations. After you are done, look at the list and mark dreams that sound everyday or don't relate to you. Reevaluate your motivation for pursuing the ones dreams and consider adjusting them to mirror your real dreams.

Your   Goals:

_____

_____

Their

Goals:_____

_____

Sometimes an extended-term purpose is surely too a long manner in the future to make revel in in your modern-day state of affairs. Even if a intention is wise and for my part pushed, if it's far too a long way down the road, it's far difficult to make it relatable to the existing 2nd. If this is the case for Neil, he may additionally moreover need to interrupt down his purpose of becoming a CEO into many smaller desires in advance than his reviews seem useful and relevant to him. It isn't that his intention of becoming a CEO is externally imposed, however turning into a CEO is to date in the destiny that month-to-month critiques seem trivial. Neil needs a goal in which his month-to-month reviews are an apparent and direct stepping-stone to success, which incorporates receiving a advertising and advertising internal his present day company. It's similar to throwing a rock right into a puddle in desire to a lake. Which do you suspect is going to make the larger splash?

If your lengthy-term goals are too big and you are finding yourself continuously dropping motivation moving ahead, first ensure that they'll be personally pushed. If they will be, spoil them down until you have got a listing of brief-time period desires which can be more relevant to your modern-day state of affairs. Doing so will make certain that your "whys" relate to who you're these days and not a far off vision of yourself.

Mantras

Regaining attention on a task can frequently be as easy as giving your self a brief pep talk and reminder approximately why you're doing the task in the first vicinity. Tell yourself to maintain shifting, to hold writing, to stop complaining, to honestly preserve going. Especially whilst walking on the ones prolonged duties which have a miles off end line, it is easy to get distracted due to the reality we've overlooked the "why." All we want is a reminder and, greater frequently than no longer, we are the tremendous humans to do it. Sometimes we're better at whipping ourselves into form than any boss, decide, pal, or coworker might be. We don't need a deep conversation probing our intentions, dreams, goals, and souls. We want a quick kick inside the pants to assist us circulate on.

In those moments while your recognition starts to wane, be organized with a brief mantra to provide that little spark of motivation and remind you of your "why." Keep it quick and particular. For instance, Neil may additionally additionally virtually recite "CEO" even as he feels his recognition on his file waning. As a runner, I tell myself to "settle in" as a reminder to calm my body and receive the ache. You might also recite the decision of a person you desire to make proud, a line from a music that pushes you more difficult, or a quote from a person you understand. Experiment with what works top notch for you and will growth your awareness on responsibilities whilst it starts offevolved to slip.

Use the space underneath to brainstorm mantras which can be massive to you. Remember that, at the same time as you can have mantras which can be inspiring on a ordinary basis, you'll in all likelihood must adapt and create new mantras to in form the desires of a given project.

Chapter 11: Visualization

Visualizations may additionally moreover furthermore appear to be a panacea promising to resolve everything from weight reduction to low vanity. Success, strength, love, friendship, wealth, happiness, peace, and sanity all magically come approximately after an remarkable dose of visualizations. So, why am I going to feature however some different spherical of them for your plate? Because they paintings. It's no mistake that experts from nutrients to agency are trying to harness the massive capability of visualization strategies. As I'm not involved together collectively with your waistline or the valuation of your begin-up, allow's start through explaining why visualization will assist you on this specific goal of developing your reputation.

When you visualize your future self, you aren't honestly devising a fictional individual. While you couldn't care that your preferred movie character misses the software program application reduce-off date for that new mission, I bet you experience in any other case whilst it's your turn. This is why we are capable of entertain ourselves for hours with imagined memories of a protracted way-off adventures but revel in unwell at the identical time because it's time to board the plane ourselves. Imagination is ready writing yourself a story that you could both placed on a highbrow bookshelf or erase. Visualization takes it a step similarly and convinces you that it's a story virtually really worth dwelling.

Visualization works for the equal purpose that remarkable reinforcement frequently works higher than punishment. Did you ever make your dad and mom proud as a infant and strive even more difficult the following time to win that identical praise?

The promise of reward is often greater appealing than the priority of results and you are much more likely to stick to a intention if you are aware of the reward you can attain from carrying out it than the penalty you will be thru falling brief. While we will talk the fee of unhappiness within the next financial disaster, right now we're involved with the energy of seeking out praise. Once you become snug visualizing the very last effects of your dreams, distractions lose their energy and look like a senseless detour from the existence you're making plans to assemble for yourself.

Visualization can produce similar feelings of pleasure, success, love, comfort, and accomplishment as having certainly completed the venture. Although fantasy, your visualizations are deeply associated with you due to the reality, well, they're you. The more potent the feelings associated with your visualizations of your future self, the greater stimulated you may revel in to have the state of affairs flip out as you intend and the an awful lot less difficult it's far going to be to push back distractions. Let's test our friend Neil to get a higher concept of the way this works.

It's nearing the stop of the month and Neil desires to publish his everyday thirty-day document to his boss. Despite Neil's suitable intentions, each month he well-knownshows himself searching at his laptop the night time in advance than the closing date with a big cup of coffee and a feel of dread constructing in his belly. Neil remains up all night writing the record and spends tomorrow barely capable of string together coherent sentences.

Now, it's apparent that this situation doesn't have to expose out this manner month after month. Neil is privy to his document closing date and might without problem are looking forward to how many hours it will take him to complete. He has a wonderful information of what his boss expects, how the report wants to be written, and what the final product should appear to be. Neil has everything he needs to prevail, but every month he waits too lengthy to start and suffers the outcomes the next day. So why can't Neil alternate his conduct? Neil desires to peer, sense, and revel in the opportunity.

Let's say that in area of waiting till the night time time earlier than the final date, Neil sits down at his table every week earlier and visualizes himself turning his record into his boss. He sees himself rested and glad. He has had an entire 8 hours of sleep, eaten a domestic made breakfast of eggs and bacon, and has even had time to iron his blouse and located on his favored tie. When he gets to the office, he talks with a coworker about the day's modern activities, responds to the e-mails prepared in his queue, and makes lunch plans along along with his partner. When his boss comes via his place of work, Neil makes a shaggy canine tale about the agency excursion party and palms over the file smartly organized in its blue presentation folder.

Neil visualizes this effective state of affairs so vividly that he can feel the experience of achievement and pleasure that it might create inside him. It is so tangible that he feels a sense of responsibility to make certain that it occurs. As Neil movements ahead for the duration of his week, he reminds himself of those first rate emotions and makes use of them as motivation to begin his report early. Whenever he is tempted to check his desired show or get lost in a net internet site on-line, Neil conjures up that feeling of accomplishment and tells himself that no longer some thing could enjoy as correct as having his imaginative and prescient end up fact.

The Bigger Picture

While it may appear excellent that Neil's procrastinating techniques may be changed via clean visualization sports activities, you'll be surprised through how motivating it's miles to view yourself as you preference to be. There is a seize, even though. Although Neil frolicked clarifying, redefining, and crafting his "why" of turning into CEO, the bigger image of his existence as a CEO isn't the food for his visualizations. While there's nothing incorrect with fantasies that artwork to validate the "whys" of your big dreams, visualizations that aren't right now related to the task to hand may be paralyzing.

There are masses of things that want to take vicinity earlier than Neil's dream of becoming a CEO can be discovered out. If he sits proper all the way down to write his file with the goal of visualizing himself as a CEO, he may be flooded with extraordinary feelings, but now not have any clean image of what his subsequent step want to be. Should he write his report or artwork on his resume? Should he reach out to his network or evaluation the time desk for the meeting he's going for walks the following day? Should he purchase the blue in form or the black one? Suddenly Neil is fed on through the entirety and a few element he'll need to do in his many-yr adventure to CEO, in choice to specializing in his modern-day record.

Becoming a CEO represents Neil's bigger picture, at the identical time as his modern difficulty is the smaller photo of writing his report. By visualizing the bigger image,

Neil gets distracted via everything he will be doing and fails to gain readability on what he ought to be doing. Despite being an essential thing of his profession development, file writing suddenly seems insignificant in contrast to the responsibilities he may want to have down the road. Who cares about month-to-month critiques after visualizing essential hundred-person groups and occupying the corner workplace? Neil is newly inspired to come to be a CEO, but his consciousness on his report is shot.

Goals and the "whys" in the back of them are designed to offer an overarching which means that and storyline to life, on the same time as visualizations are meant to inform cutting-edge-day-day conduct. Be fine that your visualizations are targeted at the task at hand and the larger image. There's extra than enough time in an afternoon to fantasize about your larger dreams. Remember the ones nineteen hours according to week left unaccounted for? When you need to advantage consciousness on a assignment, maintain your visualizations as precise as feasible. Your visualizations need to translate into direct movement, some component that acquired't display up if they amplify too a long way past the triumphing 2d.

Taking Action

As we cited, it is crucial that your visualizations are project specific and translate into direct motion. While Neil may additionally use visualization to encourage his file writing in recent times, this approach may be successfully used for any task an awful lot much less than a 12 months inside the future. Be strict approximately this 365 days cut-off date. Anything greater than a yr away has the ability to appear too distant and acquired't translate into applicable movement. It's the difference amongst imagining subsequent 12 months's Thanksgiving dinner party even as you're despite the reality that at this 12 months's celebration and imagining an aspect list for pumpkin pie because the end of October techniques. Which do you think is going to cause you to get into the car and bypass grocery buying?

Appropriate visualization have to obviously aspect in the direction of a direction of movement. If you visualize your reason and don't have any concept what to do next, you need to assume smaller and additional quick term. Neil's visualizations regarding turning into a CEO don't inform him what to do within the present 2d. I wager he might be simply as tempted to waste time on social media as he have turn out to be five minutes inside the past. On the opportunity hand, visualizations regarding completing his report on time will lead him to a very discernible route of movement—begin strolling on the document.

Use the chart below to report how your visualizations will translate into motion. Not handiest will this characteristic a reminder of methods you need to be spending it gradual at the same time as tempted thru distractions, it's going to assist you ensure that your visualizations are associated with the modern-day task and no longer the bigger photograph. If you write some issue down and cannot recall the movement it translates to, it's possibly you need to assume smaller and shorter time period.

Visualization

→

Action

_____

Connecting to the Bigger Picture

At this factor, Neil has set himself as much as have no exceptional alternative but to focus on his file. While the basketball sport can be tempting, Neil has built a robust protection closer to distractions. Let's see what he's constructed to prepare himself:

1) a vision of himself healthy, glad, and nicely rested with a completed file in his hands

2) feelings of delight, accomplishment, and pride at having met his purpose

three) knowledge of the moves he wants to take to write down his report

4) an facts of his "why" of turning into a CEO which could most effective be found out if he fulfills his first purpose of completing his report on time

Wait, wait. Didn't I just say that desires shouldn't increase beyond a one year?

Yes, your visualizations must now not boom beyond a yr, however it's herbal to your short-term desires to feature up to a bigger purpose and subsequently the bigger image and your "whys." It could be bizarre if Neil's desire to install writing a fulfillment monthly evaluations brought approximately now not whatever however an eternity of writing monthly critiques. Although visualizations want to cognizance at the undertaking at hand, it may be useful to don't forget how the mission to hand hyperlinks to your prolonged-time period dreams.

Chapter 12: Disappointment

Everyone is aware about the vintage saying that it feels higher to have someone be indignant with you than disillusioned. It seems that we might rather be yelled at, shamed, ridiculed, and thrown in a Dumpster than be knowledgeable we're disappointing. And it's proper. There are few topics extra gut-wrenching than disappointment. While you may want to stay clean of this sense, I need you to accept as genuine with me as we dive headfirst into it. Believe it or not, sadness, and reading how to enjoy it, can help a terrific deal in final targeted on a undertaking.

Let's cross lower returned to the concept of visualization for a minute. Pick a task you want to finish and in area of visualizing it going as deliberate, permit it circulate honestly wrong. Instead of making the alternatives as a manner to make you experience thrilled with your self, visualize your self doing the other. Neil, for example, will consider himself squandering away his time the night time earlier than his report is due. He will see himself spending hours on social media, getting swept up in his desired tv show and showing as heaps as work collectively with his hair uncombed. He imagines himself turning over a half of-written record to his boss and stammering whilst asked why it wasn't finished in time. Neil shall we himself experience the frustration that this sort of situation ought to cause. Instead of the feelings of success and ease that his a success visualization produced, he now feels a pit in his stomach related to his failure. I want you to experience this failure as tangibly as Neil does. Take the primary short-term motive on your listing from the preceding financial disaster and visualize yourself making horrible picks approximately it until you have were given worked up a feel you won't quick forget approximately.

The risk in visualizing unhappiness is that you may feel the emotion so tangibly that you throw the complete purpose out the window. This is why you need to complete your notable visualizations first and keep them on the the the front of your mind as you do your disappointment visualizations. Your interest is to behave due to the fact the smooth-up organization, taking every mess as it comes and right now making it safe to stroll on. The manner you do this is thru linking an event that triggers a terrible emotion to one which triggers a pleasant emotion and placing an movement object amongst them. Here is what that might look like for Neil:

1) Negative Emotion Event: preserving a half of-written file → Action Item: turning off the TV an hour in advance the night

time in advance than → Positive Emotion Event: turning in an entire record

2) Negative Emotion Event: explaining his tardiness to his boss → Action Item: turning his cellphone on silent so as no longer to pay interest the notifications → Positive Emotion Event: cracking jokes about the vacation party collectively with his boss tomorrow

What this exercise does is hyperlink contrary emotions to as a minimum one route of action, letting you notice that small alternatives must have huge affects on the manner you enjoy on the notion of a purpose. While it may seem ridiculous that turning off the TV early need to make the distinction amongst sadness and delight, I bet each person can recount a couple of story about how a 5-minute distraction grew to take over an entire night time.

Now you have have been given feelings associated with this motion item, one that makes you feel accurate and one that doesn't. The brilliant visualization ought to revel in so accurate and the terrible visualization want to enjoy so horrible that your choice to move closer to the wonderful one is inevitable and looks as if the only logical choice. If this isn't the case, you want to maintain to growth your visualizations until they are tangible sufficient to elicit this reaction.

Once you revel in comfortable with visualization, exercising switching among the extraordinary and the horrible at a 2nd's phrase and then moving on. There isn't always any advantage to this exercise if finishing it motives more distraction than the distraction you have been looking for to keep away from in the first area. Neil received't make very masses development on his record if he's spending all of his time visualizing the incredible and terrible results of his movements and in no way starting off to the commercial enterprise of writing. While it could take practice within the beginning, you need to be tempted with the aid of social media and, in a cut up 2d, be capable of experience the frustration of failing to finish your venture or the pride in completing it on time, after which be capable of get decrease again to artwork. Feel the emotions deeply, however bypass on quick. This isn't always the time to wander off in your myth destiny dreamworld. This is a motivational tool that serves to move you ahead with the subsequent step. Once you've completed your visualizations and set a foundation, best use them to get you on your cause.